Social Control

in the Colonial Economy

Social Control in the Colonial Economy

J. R. T. Hughes

University Press of Virginia

Charlottesville

THE UNIVERSITY PRESS OF VIRGINIA
Copyright © 1976 by the Rector and Visitors
of the University of Virginia

First published 1976

Library of Congress Cataloging in Publication Data

Hughes, Jonathan R T
    Social control in the colonial economy.

    Includes index.
    1. United States—Economic conditions—To 1865.
I. Title.
HC104.H83   330.9'73'02   75-17630   ISBN 0-8139-0623-7

Printed in the United States of America

Preface

This little book is the fruit of a long search. As an undergraduate, now a quarter of a century ago, I was puzzled by the way law and custom stood as constraining forces in the center of economic transactions. The logic of economic theory explained the real world only to the boundary line of law, whose logic, when not mysterious altogether, was certainly in many ways alien to the economic way of thinking. Why the law should be so was left unexplained in our books apart from observations about morals, politics, and ideas of justice. They clearly were not enough. Why, for example, should some businesses be legal only if licensed by civil authority and others legal without specific license? What justified government controls?

As my specialty became economic history, I had occasion to note that in different times the law, although always there, played varying roles. A given kind of economic transaction might be controlled at one time and free of control, in the same objective circumstances, at another date in history. Beyond American history under the Federal Constitution the colonial background loomed as *terra incognita*. It was always said to be the remote source of our laws and customs, but it was mysterious. The very words were foreign. What was socage? What was glebeland? What was a market overt? Why did colonial Americans have such things, and where did they go? Why did they disappear? By 1970 my interest in the record of social control imposed by the laws of the republic had finally led me to Francis Newton Thorpe's great collection of colonial documents and state constitutions. It was at that point, during a year largely spent in Northwestern University's Deering Library, wondering about the remote implications of such things as Lord Baltimore's right to establish view of frankpledge granted in Maryland's charter of 1632, that I determined to "bite the bullet," to push my research back the necessary centuries, into the necessary places, and try to learn the relevant language and customs of colonial America and its Britannic ancestor.

The work in this volume depends heavily upon research in 1971-72, done in the Codrington Library during my term as a Visiting Fellow of All Souls College, Oxford. I wish to thank the Warden and Fellows of the College for their hospitality and conversation and the Ford Foundation for its support. My colleagues at Northwestern, Lacey Smith and Timothy Breen, gave me the benefit of their advice. To my colleague, Eric Jones, now of La Trobe University, my gratitude for patience and several years of running discussion about England and English and colonial American institutions. In Oxford, my thanks to Professor Anthony Honoré for advice on certain problems of legal interpretation; to John Simmons, the erudite librarian of the Codrington, for general encouragement and help; and to Professor Geoffrey Barraclough for help with matters mainly medieval and legal. As is customary, I absolve them all of any blame for the failings these chapters may contain. It is also customary in a scholarly book to credit the inspiration of great teachers, if one had any. I did. When I was an undergraduate student at the Utah State Agricultural College, Professor Evan Murray taught me about the intermingling of law and economics in such a way that the subject remained in my head through all the years when I pursued other interests. The material in this little book thus brings part of my education full circle.

Since some might say that by writing this book I have abandoned my last, economic history, let me add a caveat: the rules of economic behavior imposed by society at large are not irrelevant to the way such a society develops. The proper study of economic development should embrace all the relevant information, not just the numerical artifacts of the past. I intend that this book will help to add a new dimension to American economic history, the original character of social control imposed through law and government.

Evanston, Illinois
1975

Contents

Part I

Social Control and Social Institutions in Economic Life

1
Introduction

This book is an examination of nonmarket controls over economic life in our country's formative years. The colonial experience is more than a mere prologue to modern American history; it is the wellspring of our separate existence as a nation, and nowhere more than in our tradition and practice of nonmarket control over economic life.

When, in August 1971, Richard Nixon revealed a new galaxy of direct measures of government intervention in the economy as his proposed solutions to our problems, the economic historian had a weary feeling of *déjà vu*. The record in American history of currency manipulation and price and wage controls is a very lengthy one, centuries old, and is not particularly inspiring as a catalogue of wisdom. Still, the historian's professional spirit was buoyed up by a sudden sense of relevance; his knowledge of the past was usable. He knew that the statesmen of the early 1970s were standing squarely in the mainstream of national folly and were not embarking upon new and untried experiments. We had all been there before.

The rights of government to intervene in price and wage determination comprise a small part of ancient social control powers over economic life in Anglo-American law and custom. These rights were written down in Magna Carta, and whatever can be said for their wisdom, there is no question of their legitimacy. Our economic system is enfolded in a larger social fabric, and legal economic activities, in the end, are those which are consistent with the usages of that larger social fabric. The kind, or mix, of social controls over economic activity that exists at different points in history varies. The potential range is from the total command economy to the essential absence of positive government influence. In the former case economic life is made to reflect the objects of state policy without regard to the resource allocations that would result if the play of the forces of demand and supply in the market were to prevail. Both sorts of policies are social control over economic life, nonmarket and market social control. The price mechanism is, after all, as much a social control device as is a central-planning system. The difference is that the price mechanism allocates resources according to the desires of buyers and sellers while a planning system allocates resources in aid of whatever forces create the plans. If prices produced by the free market allocate resources, the social control is according to consumer desires and is market social control. If law, custom, or agencies of government intervene and create a different allocation for reasons not related to current market conditions, or to thwart them, then the social control is nonmarket.

Ultimately the legitimacy of any economic system must be judged by the objectives of the surrounding social organism. Any kind of system can apparently succeed or fail to produce the desired consequences of policy, whether that policy be economic development and growth or social stability with economic stasis. There is no single kind of economic system which has been favored by the makers and shakers of history in all circumstances.

The long English and American tradition has been a pragmatic one of variations in the mix of market and nonmarket social control in connection with the circumstances of social and economic change. There are essentially four elements of economic life over which our society has variously changed the mix of social control: (1) the number of participants allowed, (2) the conditions of eligibility for participation, (3) the prices charged by participants for their services or production, and (4) the quality of services and products allowed. If these four elements are given values of 1 or 0, depending upon whether the social control mechanism is nonmarket (government regulation) or market (the price system), there are sixteen pure forms possible in successive permutations.

1. [(1) one participant, (2) entry restricted, (3) price regulated, (4) quality regulated]

    .
    .
    .

.
.
.

16. [(1) any number, (2) entry unrestricted, (3) prices unregulated, (4) quality unregulated] [1]

The first example is a strictly controlled monopoly (say a royal mint), the last is economic freedom with the price mechanism as the social control. Between the extremities are fourteen combinations of licensing, inspection systems, franchises, and direct price and wage control—essentially the whole world of degrees of government regulation that are at all levels of government our way of economic life. Historically all forms have been present in Anglo-American society simultaneously, and the student of social control learns to recognize the various permutations in the historical evidence. For example, a modern town might allow considerable variability in (1), (3), and (4) in such cases as barber shops, but (2) is usually regulated by license; (1) (3), and (4) are usually left to the price mechanism in land ownership, but (2) involves title search, and deed, so entry is restricted. Also liens, easements, and other reservations specified may place restrictions upon (4), quality. Strict control usually exists in all four in cases like hotels and taverns. Number (3), price, is usually left to the price mechanism for such institutions as hospitals, nursing homes, and sanatoriums. Farming (land ownership itself apart) before the AAA or labor contracts before the Wagner Act and the Fair Labor Standards Act are usually given as examples where the price mechanism customarily controlled all four. Clearly society faces a wide range of policy alternatives in its social control choices, and American society has changed a great deal over time in its approach to these options. The pattern of that change is the greatest issue facing the American economy today—the tendency for

---

[1] The sixteen permutations, valued 0 and 1, are

(1)	(1)	(1)	(1)	(0)	(1)	(1)	(1)
(1)	(1)	(1)	(0)	(0)	(0)	(1)	(1)
(1)	(1)	(0)	(0)	(0)	(0)	(0)	(1)
(1)	(0)	(0)	(0)	(0)	(1)	(0)	(0)
(1)	(0)	(1)	(1)	(0)	(0)	(1)	(0)
(1)	(1)	(0)	(1)	(0)	(1)	(0)	(1)
(1)	(0)	(1)	(0)	(0)	(1)	(1)	(0)
(1)	(0)	(0)	(1)	(0)	(0)	(0)	(0)

the country continuously to be nudged up against the first option, total regulation by our government officials. A fifth method of control, quantitative—direct control of output levels—has been only a rare occurrence in Anglo-American history, mainly limited to wartime and similar emergencies.

The concern of this study is with the original choices made by the English and their American colonial enterprises in the century and a half before the American Revolution. The subject is of great importance for any understanding of America's subsequent history, including that of our own era, a time when nonmarket control has reached proportions reminiscent of the colonial era. It was, after all, the government nonmarket control apparatus of eighteenth-century English mercantilism that Adam Smith attacked in the *Wealth of Nations* in the same year, 1776, that Americans declared their independence of it. We were then English, with variations, and that apparatus became the basis of our own practice after independence was achieved, and continues to the present time. England was the original seedbed for the modern American exfoliation of nonmarket social control.

But one should not study the century and a half of colonial America limited entirely by modern notions of rationality in economic life. Some activities like communal gardening made more sense when elementary survival itself was at stake than they would today. In the planting and development of the early colonies one sees nothing less than the formation of American society. What was appropriate then may not seem entirely rational to the modern mind. The English laws, customs, and practices were the original materials, to be transmuted slowly by American experience into the American way of life; that is, they were made to conform to American realities to some extent. But we were and are a common-law country, so the influence of past experience shapes our development continually. Extreme change is difficult to achieve in law, and in any case, originality in social policy is far more rare than one might imagine. Maintaining government control over businesses and insisting upon public obligations of corporations and public utilities, local responsibility for the poor, payment of property taxes upon pain of losing property outright for the amount of the unpaid taxes—all such practices are long-term exercises in Anglo-American historical experience, not matters of logic alone.

All societies have rules regarding economic activity. They must, even at the family level, or else no orderly and sustained social fabric could exist. Even the purest form of economic freedom involves consent by the other members of society, and man being what he is, that consent must be enforceable. Thus the modern doyen of nineteenth-century liberalism, Milton Friedman, began his celebrated essay, *Capitalism and Freedom,* with the assertion: "Government is necessary to preserve our freedom."[2] Once that proposition is accepted, however, the camel's nose is inside the tent, and the question then arises, how much government? Americans are routinely taught the Jeffersonian value judgment, "That government is best which governs least." Even if it be assumed that we all agree about what the word "best" means, we are still left with "least," and the definition of that word is a matter of continuing dispute.

The following chapters set forth the reason for the dispute as it emerges from this country's earliest economic history. At the time of the first colonies, the early seventeenth century, English institutions were undergoing widespread upheaval in the wake of the Elizabethan era's commercial surge. James I granted Virginia its charter, and Charles I was in power when the Massachusetts Bay Colony was founded only a decade before the "mighty storm" of the Puritan revolution, as R. H. Tawney put it. Our first institutions of economic control came out of that maelstrom, partly feudal, partly monarchical, partly republican. There never was a pure model to be corrupted by use; instead, usage of an institutional collage of social theories gave us the experience to develop our own notions of such pure intellectual forms as free enterprise. In our case, art followed nature, slowly.

The material we will examine in the pages below will come as something of a shock to those economists and historians who think that our modern techniques of economic control are products of the mind of man in the technotronic society and that in some happier golden age and place, called colonial America, free markets allocated resources. Some dogmatists may persist in the belief that Adam Smith was wrong in attacking the mercantilist system, that the eighteenth-century English-speaking world was

[2]Chicago, 1962, p. 2.

really a hotbed of laissez faire, and that systems of control over economic activity such as those framed to govern colonial America somehow must have been ineffective. Such beliefs are rooted in the idea that what is illogical in simple economic theory will some-how be disregarded and fall of its own accord. Nothing could be further from the truth, as should be clear to anyone considering our own modern laws governing economic activity in this country. The logic of economic theory and what Chancellor James Kent called "the policy of the law" have no necessary connection. Nevertheless, some will persist in the belief that colonial America was a place where competitive prices were achieved by the free market and prevailed in the allocation of resources, despite the mass of legal and customary barriers to such a consummation. If anything could be, this book should be an antidote to such beliefs.

2
The Colonial Crucible:
General Considerations

The right of individual freedom subject to universally accepted nonmarket social control has been a, central theme in our economic history from the Jamestown settlement to President Nixon's "economy of phases" in 1971-74. One cannot foresee an end to this trend, and its historic root is located in the colonial experience and even beyond. To understand how we use the instruments of nonmarket social control, the powers of government, legislation, and regulation, involves us in a practical use of history. Today's new departures can be seen as new applications of established precedents. The problems have come up again and again.

Intrinsically we seem to recognize that the past matters in contemporary life, and we expect historians to tell us why. How much does history matter? What parts matter most, and what parts least? It is obviously not the case that the more remote in time a given historical episode lies, the less relevant it is as a determinant of the course of events. Euclid's geometry is a good example in the history of ideas, and one could even turn to geologic history and see how events of eons ago determine the course of daily economic and political life as seen in the latest newspapers. The usefulness of history depends upon current needs; and these determine to a large extent what questions we ask of history. Thus the usefulness of history changes day by day. But its everyday utility can hardly be measured, except in cases like geology and the law, where the past impinges directly upon us. In the general realms of ideas and culture, the usefulness of historical study is less readily comprehended.

It is for this reason that most modern Americans are not directly interested in the English colonies in America. We are only dimly aware of our European background; the American Revolution and the appearance in 1789 of a written constitution seem to have put a full stop to our English past. Similarly, memory of the

French and Spanish influence in Louisiana, Florida, and the Southwest has faded, apart from such reminders as certain anomalies in the law, the more pleasant tourist attractions, and the cultural and linguistic heritage of the two countries. From the federal period forward in American history one speaks of familiar things, for example, the Supreme Court and the doctrine of judicial review, the role of public utilities and their regulation. We know these things. The words describe a concrete reality, burning everyday issues, and are thus congenial to the mind. But there is an intellectual veil between the Constitution and what went before. Such terms as the Board of Trade or the law of public callings, which a historian uses in describing the instances of review of laws and nonmarket social control in the American colonies, seem strange, foreign. By changes in language our own history drifts suddenly out of reach.

Similarly, we can reconcile the modern idea of real property held in absolute fee simple with the authority of our various political units to seize it and sell it for taxes. Yet the idea that another American government, a proprietary power, the Lords Baltimore in Maryland or the Penns of Pennsylvania, might have done the same for nonpayment of taxes called quitrents seems an outrage against common sense, which fortunately was ended by the Revolution. Lands could escheat, or return, to the feudal lord for failure to perform the conditions of tenure—payment of taxation or failure of heirs. Yet they do the same in our several governmental jurisdictions today. The Virginia Constitution of 1776 was clear enough about this point: "All escheats, penalties, and forfeitures, heretofore going to the King, shall go to the Commonwealth, save only such as the legislature may abolish, or otherwise provide for."[1] As the great legal scholar James Bradley Thayer put it: "The Revolution came, and then what happened? Simply this: we cut the cord that tied us to Great Britain, and there was no longer an external sovereign. Our conception now was that 'the people' took his place. . . . so far as existing institutions were left untouched, they were construed by translating the

---

[1]Francis Newton Thorpe, ed., *The Federal and State Constitutions, Colonial Charters, and Other Organic Laws of the States, Territories, and Colonies Now or Heretofore Forming the United States of America* (Washington, D.C., 1909), p. 3818.

name and style of the English sovereign into that of our new ruler—ourselves, the People."[2] The procedures of social organization relating to economic and social life continued through the changes of words following 1789 to an astonishing degree, and American history has been stripped of part of its own richness, of the means by which it might be understood, by the changes in nomenclature that came with independence. As a result, we commonly attribute a degree of singularity and native originality to our institutional structure which is not justified.

In many cases the gaps in our history due to changes of language are of surprising antiquity. The pictures of wanted fugitives at the local post office, the transfer of prisoners and public charges between local political and legal jurisdictions, both hark back to the hue and cry of colonial practice. Those laws, in turn, were but adaptations of the King's Peace and the Statute of Winchester of 1285, when King Edward I placed the responsibility for law and order directly upon his subjects—with monetary penalties for failure. The king was, of course, merely codifying even older customs. Thus to see the same provisions in the Massachusetts laws of 1660 is indeed like seeing a ghost.[3]

Similarly, American towns and cities long practiced local controls over markets,[4] both by specifying location and days and hours of provender and by setting up controls over the qualities and measurements of goods and services sold therein. In colonial times such practices were nearly universal,[5] and they had even more ancient English roots in the freedom of towns to establish such markets overt and in the power of the unique institution of the law merchant, or commercial law, the courts of piepoudre, to determine the rules of trade. Commercial law thus had an ancient place separate from the jurisdiction of the courts of common

---

[2]*Legal Essays* (Cambridge, Mass., 1927), p. 4.

[3]The Statute of Winchester is printed in J. J. Bagley and P. B. Rowley, *A Documentary History of England* (London, 1966); pp. 158-60 concern this method of law enforcement. The Massachusetts hue and cry appears in a law of 1646 (William Whitmore, ed., *The Colonial Laws of Massachusetts* [Boston, 1889], pp. 139-40).

[4]The practice is traced briefly into the frontier by Richard Wade, "Urban Life in Western America, 1790-1830," *American Historical Review* 54 (1958): 20.

[5]See ch. 9 below.

law.[6] The clerks and wardens of the American markets of the early nineteenth century had not only their colonial forebears but, by continuity, more ancient ancestors as well. Thus the 1691 charter of Philadelphia, in the general power it gives clerks of the market to regulate the prices of such items as beer, bread, and wine and to impose standard weights and measures, restates the same powers guaranteed in Magna Carta.[7] When, in 1846, the citizens of New York excised these ancient constraints from their new constitution by decreeing that "all offices for the weighing, gauging, measuring, culling or inspecting any merchandize, produce, manufacture or commodity, whatever, are hereby abolished, and no such office shall hereafter be created by law,"[8] they overthrew, with some exceptions, not only the colonial legacy of consumer protection but a far older legacy as well. The citizens of the Empire State have more recently changed their course on these issues.

In no area is the continuity of colonial and modern history more striking than that of nonmarket social control of economic life, from consumer protection to the fundamental rules of ownership and control of productive resources. The citizen wants protection from the logical consequences of the free market, whenever it hurts him, and the fundamental continuity of the law provides the vehicle. There is abundant precedent, for the problem has been coterminous with free markets themselves—a fact perhaps painful to some economists but nonetheless evident in legal history.[9] How we have conducted those social relations arising from economic activity has been, apart from piracy and theft, the subject of constraint by law, both statute and common. Even the framers of the Sherman Antitrust Act of 1890 claimed a common-law warrant.[10]

[6]See pp. 126-32 below.

[7]Edward P. Allinson and Boies Penrose, *Philadelphia, 1681-1887* (Baltimore, 1887), p. xlix; Magna Carta, art. 35, in Bagley and Rowley, p. 106.

[8]Thorpe, p. 2662.

[9]Karl Polanyi, in *The Great Transformation* (Boston, 1957), argues strongly that an uncontrolled market would reduce human beings intolerably (see, e.g., p. 73). From medieval times, in the West, markets were controlled by the boroughs and towns and their guilds.

[10]William Letwin, *Law and Economic Policy in America* (New York, 1965), ch. 2.

Our statutes rarely have been utterly original, since our social organism has had a real continuity, despite changes of vocabulary, and old habits linger. But the law also reinforces these habits. The words and clauses of our present-day deeds of conveyance are thought to be of Saxon origin, and so the rules regarding such matters as distraint of property as security for debt.[11] The rules of contract, the rights of property in hereditaments of all sorts, our common understanding regarding conditions of sale, lease, or hire, the obligations of workmen and their employees—all these and hundreds more of the most common social transactions of every-day life are rooted in the laws of our ancestors and have been transmitted with small enough change over the centuries because of the logic, as well as the justice, of the vast corpus of behavioral rules which form the common and statute laws of peoples of English origin.

In colonial times the laws passed by the assemblies in the colonies were closely watched by the lawyers of the Board of Trade to see that they were not repugnant to the laws of "this our realm of England," at least "as near as may be." From 1696, when the board was established, to 1776 some four hundred of these laws were disallowed by this form of judicial review.[12] It was settled doctrine that the whole of the English common law together with all statutes passed in England before colonization automatically formed the basic law in every colony.[13] To this

[11] James Kent, *Commentaries on American Law*, 12th ed., ed. O. W. Holmes, Jr. (Boston, 1873), 4:500, on deeds, and 3:631 n.6, on distraint for debt among the Saxons.

[12] Oliver Morton Dickerson, *American Colonial Government, 1696-1765* (Cleveland, 1912), p. 227. Charles G. Haines, *The American Doctrine of Judicial Supremacy* (Berkeley, Calif., 1932) ch. 1, n.1, puts the number at 469 out of a total of 8,563 acts of colonial assemblies examined by the Board of Trade. The process of judicial review previously exercised by the crown was discussed at the Constitutional Convention of 1787 (*Documents Illustrative of the Formation of the Union of the American States* [Washington, D.C., 1927], pp. 174-79). The constraint appeared very early. In the ordinance for Virginia of July 24-Aug. 3, 1621, empowering the Virginia House of Burgesses, no law made by the general assembly was to be law unless "ratified and confirmed, in a General Quarter Court of the said Company here in England" (Thorpe, p. 3812). See also Roscoe Pound, "The Development of American Law and Its Deviation from English Law," *Law Quarterly Review* 67 (1951): 158-59.

[13] The charters gave full rights as native-born Englishmen to the colonists. James I, in the Virginia Charter of 1606, said that the prospective colonists "shall have and enjoy all

were added laws passed by Parliament explicitly extending to the colonies, together with those laws, like the Statute of Frauds of Charles II, which the colonial assemblies adopted outright.[14] Indeed, the Continental Congress in 1774 claimed the common law of England and the statutes up to the time of colonization.[15] When the Revolution came, the states of Massachusetts, New York, New Jersey, Delaware, and Maryland wrote constitutions that simply adopted the major corpus of English law and passed it straight into the life of the new nation,[16] except, turning the worm, as the New York document stated, those parts which might

Liberties, Franchises and Immunities, within any of our other Dominions . . . as if they had been abiding and born, within this our Realm of England" (Thorpe, p. 3788). Originally this extension of English law was meant to protect the colonists from abuses of local government. Hence the colonists correctly believed themselves to be entitled to the rights of Englishmen. See Thomas Jefferson, *Notes on the State of Virginia* (London, 1788), p. 218. Jefferson was of the opinion that the common law and all the abstract law up to 1607 was in force in Virginia, together with statutes extended to Virginia after 1607. For the same view in New England, see *The Literary Diary of Ezra Stiles*, ed. Franklin B. Dexter (New York, 1901), 1:331. See also Richard B. Morris, "Massachusetts and the Common Law: The Declaration of 1646," *American Historical Review* 31 (1925-26): 443. Morris held that, contrary to the case the Puritans were trying to make, the evidence is against the idea that Massachusetts had imported the common law wholesale. Blackstone, oddly enough, argued that wherever Englishmen went to lands "desert and uncultivated," they carried with them the common law, as it was applicable. But in the American colonies, acquired by conquest, the common law of England was not valid. Blackstone is sometimes cited erroneously to support the view that English common law was imported automatically with the colonists. He thought not (William Blackstone, *Commentaries on the Laws of England* [New York, 1840], bk. 1, p. 77). The royal charters say it was, and various state legislatures said it was too. For a survey of early American opinion in law, see Kent, 1:537-38. The subject is obviously a deep one. The authority of the English common law in American practice was expressed at least once from the bench of the Supreme Court, in *Robinson* v. *Campbell*, 3 Wheaton 212 (1818), in a dispute over land titles between Virginia and Tennessee: "the remedies in the courts of the United States are to be, at common law or equity, not according to the practice of the state courts, but according to the principles of common law and equity, as distinguished and defined in that country from which we derive our knowledge of those principles" An excellent discussion of the whole issue, including the cases where the new American states explicitly rejected English citations, is found in René David and John E. C. Brierly, *Major Legal Systems in the World Today* (London, 1968), pp. 336-80.

[14]See below, p. 82.

[15]*Documents Illustrative of the Formation of the Union*, "Declarations and Resolves of the First Continental Congress, Oct. 14, 1774," pp. 1-5.

[16]Kent, 1: 537-38.

be "repugnant to this constitution."[17] In Connecticut the old royal charter of 1662, with a bill of rights attached, was made the constitution in 1776; Rhode Island's colonial charter served far into the nineteenth century, until 1842.[18]

It is not surprising that a people would shun bold departures from a way of life already a century and a half old and a body of settled law and usages congenial to their lives and customs. The fifteen decades of the colonial experience were decades of achievement mutually shared between the colonies and the mother country. The issue came up dramatically in American constitutional law in 1819, in *Dartmouth College* v. *Woodward*.[19] As Chief Justice Marshall argued, a mere revolution had not given to the sovereign state of New Hampshire powers which Parliament did not have before. To be sure, the corporation patented by King George III as Dartmouth College was "an artificial being, invisible, intangible, and existing only in contemplation of law."[20] But the legislature could not tamper with this patent; a contract in English law was a contract in the same law—now American, and not to be trifled with by the political consequences of a mere revolution. As Marshall put it: "It is too clear to require the support of argument that all contracts, and rights, respecting property, remained unchanged by the revolution."[21] His colleague, Justice Story, was equally adamant, if even more original, saying it was a settled "principle of the common law that the division of an empire works no forfeiture on previously vested rights of property," and he considered the suggestion "monstrous"[22] that the Revolution might have disturbed charters granted by the previous government, i.e., the British crown. Daniel Webster, representing the college, cut into the pretensions of the former revolutionaries smartly: "The legislature of New-Hampshire has no more power over the

---

[17]Thorpe, p. 2636.   [18]Thayer, p. 4

[19]4 Wheaton 518. Although this is thought to be the definitive case testing the contract clause of the Constitution, there was an earlier, but not so useful, case, *Fletcher v. Peck*, 6 Cranch 87 (1810).

[20]4 Wheaton 636. These words still ring through discussions of corporate law.
[21]Ibid., p. 651.   [22]Ibid., p. 707.

rights of the plaintiffs than existed, somewhere, in some depart-
ment of the government, before the revolution. The British parliament could not have annulled or revoked this grant as an act of
ordinary legislation."[23]

The student of American history knows that the justices made
the doctrine of *Dartmouth College* v. *Woodward* the definitive test
of the U.S. Constitution's contract clause. But sovereignty of contract was an ancient English idea, imbedded in colonial life, and
the Court's review of the New Hampshire legislature's act was a
product of the colonial experience. The two went together, then,
and the consequences of judicial review have been fundamental
forces in American history since. Judicial review of legislative acts
was foreign to the English constitution per se, although Sir
Edward Coke had argued in the seventeenth century that the
crown had no authority to sponsor legislation which contravened
the common law. But the colonial experience was not entirely
English, it was American as well, and the habit learned in the
decades of colonial life was passed on into the mainstream of the
new republic's life through John Marshall's decision in *Marbury* v.
Madison, in which he asserted the Court's right to review even acts
of Congress, the federal legislature.[24] Similarly, it has been suggested that the power given Congress to regulate commerce among
the states was no more than a recognition of the governmental
virtues of that power as exercised by the Board of Trade and the
vice admiralty courts during the colonial era,[25] although the uses
of the commerce clause in modern times to extend the central
power of government would no doubt have astonished even Coke,
who fought against the High Court of Admiralty in the seventeenth century precisely because he thought it endangered the
prerogatives of the common law.[26] Whatever the correct balance

[23] Ibid., pp. 558-59.

[24] 1 Cranch 137 (1803). Charles A. and Mary R. Beard, in *The Rise of American
Civilization* (New York, 1927), 1:339, state that carrying final appeals to the U.S.
Supreme Court was "just as to London in colonial times."

[25] Beard and Beard, 1 : 202-3; Charles M. Andrews, *The Colonial Period in American
History: England's Commercial and Colonial Policy* (New Haven, 1938), p. 224;
Dickerson, pp. 249-51.

[26] Andrews, p. 224.

of interpretation, it is clear that the American colonists were well aware of the power of government to regulate commerce between the colonies and with foreign nations.

Not that the law was always successful in stemming the aspirations and needs of the time. In *Dartmouth College* v. *Woodward,* the law, and not public enthusiasm as embodied in the New Hampshire legislature, prevailed; in the 1840s, in more desperate circumstances, the popular prodebtor stop laws of the Midwest requiring land to be accepted as settlement for money debts were overturned by a judiciary following the dictates of legal doctrine that land should not be forced upon creditors.[27] In other times though, the law was bent, changed, or circumvented. In colonial times, to satisfy English creditors, titles to estates seized for debt were allowed to pass, contrary to the common law of England.[28] In the Granger cases of the 1870s, the Supreme Court reached back to the seventeenth century to find common law regarding the regulation of business which served the needs of the times,[29] and in the 1930s the Supreme Court simply reversed itself, it appears, in the face of raw political power. But mainly the law has been a conservative force, both in colonial times and later.

For the future of colonial history, the reality embodied in the opinions of *Dartmouth College* v. *Woodward* was not primarily the test of the contract clause but the assurance that property rights developed before 1776, even under the seals of George III, were not going to be overthrown by revolution. As we will see presently, clarification of property rights in real estate, tangible and intangible, was an outcome of colonial experience with economic development, of simplifications of feudal usages, and of modifications to suit the needs of the New World, and the safeguard and expression of these rights formed law itself.

It is not surprising that the Supreme Court would not annul all this heritage. If the letters patent of Dartmouth College could be

---

[27]The stop, or stay, laws were passed by Ohio, Pennsylvania, Delaware, and Indiana in the 1830s and by Illinois and Michigan in 1841 (Kent, 4:443-61).

[28]5 George II, c. 7. The law reduced colonial real estate to the status of personal property, which could be seized and sold for debts owed to subjects living in Britain (Kent, 4: 443-44). Americans, in laws of 1696 in Massachusetts and 1700 and 1705 in Pennsylvania, already allowed real estate to be seized and sold for debt.

[29]See ch. 12 below.

overthrown, what of property rights in all the colonies, rights derived from the king, one of his corporate creatures, or one of his feudal vassals? If the general impact of this attitude was conservative, a society uniquely rooted in private property was not less so. And it can hardly be argued that a court upholding the sanctity of private property was acting against the interests of the people who had carried their brand of civilization into the American wilderness precisely in order to win and use the fruits of private ownership. From Maine to Georgia, and far inland, the property of Dartmouth College was of fundamental importance. Men cultivated land, towns and cities existed, wharves and bridges, roads and ferries were built, mines dug, waters navigated, a native people was disinherited and an African one enslaved—all on the accepted right of England's king to his feudal authority. He had the absolute title in England and could devise it as he pleased, according to any one of the several kinds of tenure. The colonial experience set the new nation in the direction it has traveled since. This experience is therefore worth considering in some detail.

How the land was owned, who owned it, by what right, how it was to be settled, where towns would be, what their powers would be, how business would be conducted, what was forbidden, what allowed, what free, what regulated, what would be grown and traded, who would do the labor, and under what terms, how much they would govern themselves locally, how much they were to be governed by central power, who controlled external trade, how internal trade was to be regulated—all these questions did not need to be answered anew at the end of the Revolution. The achievement of the colonial American had been nothing less than the establishment of a basic structure of social life. So the relevance of the colonial years is nothing less than the bricks and mortar of elementary historical understanding insofar as the American economy is concerned. It is not an expendable luxury, a detour from the mainstream, but the source of the mainstream itself.

In the following chapters we will examine the terms of the original settlements, the patents of the colonies (their constitutions), the laws and ordinances of those early governments. We will see an economy and society with the thick infrastructure of a settled social being. Indeed, the evidence indicates that the frontier of post-Revolutionary America was probably far more thinly structured with effective social institutions than was the colonial seaboard from almost the beginning of its existence. In the extreme case, shown by the early statutes of Massachusetts, it might well be arguable whether there is, even today, more non-market social control of economic activity than there was then. The small army of colonial selectmen and their appointees—viewers, searchers, wardens, constables, informers, keepers of the night watch and ward, sealers of weights, measures, and casks, clerks of the market—and the rules of behavior, from the rights of clammers to regulation of roaming stone-horses, must have produced as thoroughgoing a set of nonmarket controls over economic and social life as any modern government controls enthusiast could hope for. Some of it was doubtless peculiar to Massachusetts and gave the Puritan heritage a set of teeth daunting to imagine. But some of that system was common to English colonists everywhere, in law and in practice, not only in the friendlier and less theologically rigid climes of Pennsylvania and Virginia but even in tropical Bermuda, where the English settlers in the seventeenth century, "like all their race, so soon as they got anything like established they proceeded to hold courts and have election and canvass for votes, and generally to introduce all the paraphernalia of the Common Law, land tenure, primogeniture, courts, juries, sheriffs, parsons, hangmen, clerks, glebes, tipstaves, constables, vestrymen, overseers, sidesmen, bailiffs, estates tail and fee simple, Common Law and Equity Courts of original appellate jurisdiction, and all within an area of nineteen and one-half square miles."[30]

As Sumner Powell noted in his *Puritan Village*, the apparatus of English nonmarket control appeared along with the common law when the new settlements left the earliest experimental and survival states and the arrival of new generations made a settled frame of reference necessary.[31] They recreated as a base the relevant

[30]T. M. Dill, "Colonial Development of the Commonlaw," *Law Quarterly Review*, 40 (1924): 288.

[31]Sumner Chilton Powell, *Puritan Village: The Formation of a New England Town* (Middletown, Conn., 1963), ch. 10.

parts of the English mold. Then the process of change, ongoing in England, resumed its course.

The colonial world was a crucible. After the Revolution, American experience at first moved away from it into a less structured existence. But since the Civil War, perhaps the greatest single act of government interference with private business in this country's history, nonmarket social control of economic life has been continually expanding, for good or ill. It is not this author's intention to praise or decry this movement at this point, but to show in the chapters that follow how the colonial experience became of lasting importance to the American economy. Plowing under the little pigs in the 1930s, crop and acreage controls today may be seen as reruns of the Virginia assembly's efforts in 1639, by ordering the destruction of all inferior tobacco and half of the good, to raise prices by creating legal scarcity.[32] The colonial past is always with us.

---

[32]Philip A. Bruce, *Economic History of Virginia in the Seventeenth Century* (New York, 1896), pp. 323-34.

Part II

The Land: Who Shall Own?

3

The Background of Tenures

All which landes, Countreis, and territories, shall for ever be holden of the said *Walter Ralegh,* his heires and assignes, of us, our heires and successors, by homage and by the said paiment of the said fift part, reserved onely for all services.

Queen Elizabeth's Charter to Sir Walter Raleigh, 1584

Social control over property rights in land is fundamental to the coherence of any community. In modern times site and land-use laws prevail in most of our organized communities. There are no American communities now where both the number of property-right holders and entry into real estate ownership are unrestricted by law, since property rights must be confirmed by valid title. Price is still left to the market mechanism in most cases, but the quality of the property right delivered, the uses to which land may be put, is now severely restricted by zoning, licensing, and environmental controls. In nineteenth century America such restrictions were less evident because the great empty continent west of the Appalachians was treated largely as a "free good." Whole forests were wiped out, mines promiscuously exhausted, species of animals and birds massacred out of existence. The memory of those palmy days is usually called up in discussions of modern property restrictions. The restrictions of the earlier American society on property rights in land are less well known, even though our present system of land ownership evolved directly from them.

Understanding the colonial system is complicated by two factors: (1) the original property rights were descended from the social control system of medieval England, and (2) gradual piecemeal innovations in those rights occurred in the several colonies and left us with a patchwork which varied by state and by even smaller jurisdictions. Nevertheless, the English background must be examined if we are to comprehend the colonial origins of our own system.

Reverting now to the analysis in chapter 1, it will be helpful to bear in mind that the land policy of medieval England was developed by a tightly organized oligarchy which it was designed to maintain. The tightest stitches, for example, primogeniture and entailment of major estates, have rarely been equaled by any other society in devising a long-distance social control of real property. In land ownership, the number of property rights in medieval England was limited by the status or the tenure of the land owned. Entry was controlled by the requirements and rites of admission to the tenure. Price was constrained by the conditions, or incidents (payments, real and monetary, both fixed and uncertain, due to others in the future), attached to the tenures. And the quality of ownership was restricted by the external demands other property holders could place upon an individual right. In the feudal chain of property rights, the fruits, uses, and abuses of property were never free of the policy of the community at large. The system was complex, but as Blackstone said of it, "it is impossible to understand, with any degree of accuracy, either the civil constitution of this kingdom, or the laws which regulate its landed property, without some general acquaintance with the nature and doctrine of feuds, or the feudal law."[1] For our purposes only one part of the feudal system, the tenure of free and common socage, is directly relevant. It was the only tenure the American colonists were allowed by their charters. This limitation had immense practical consequences; it guaranteed that land would be used productively or sold off, and not held in great blocs as the idle estates of a landed aristocracy—a point noted by Adam Smith: "But in all the English colonies the tenure of the lands, which are all held by free socage, facilitates alienation, and the grantee of any extensive tract of land, generally finds it for his interest to alienate, as fast as he can, the greater part of it, reserving only a small quit rent."[2]

Since the first act of colonization was the acquisition, settlement, and division of the land, the tenure of property rights in

[1]*Commentaries*, Bk. 2, p. 44.

[2]*The Wealth of Nations* (New York, 1937), bk. 4, ch. 7, p. 539.

land is where our investigation begins. Queen Elizabeth granted lands not even known, by her authority as the English monarch. She gave Raleigh the land "every part in fee-simple or otherwise, according to the lawes of England, as neere as conveniently may be . . . reserving always to us our heires, and successors for all services, duties, and demaundes, a fift part of all the oare of golde and silver . . . that shal be there gotten and obtained."[3] Raleigh's charter and the Roanoke plantation came to nothing in the end, as did the charter of Sir Humphrey Gilbert before him, granted in 1578. Henry VII had given a similar charter to John Cabot in 1496 and another to Richard Warde, Thomas Ashehurst, and their associates in 1501. In those charters, as in Raleigh's, the grant of lands in fee simple meant that patentees and their heirs owned the property rights in perpetuity, so long as the conditions of the grant were fulfilled. After 1540 fee simple implied also certain rights to devise property by will. Fee simple lands could be sold and resold, each time in fee simple.[4] But most important, the grant to "heires and assignes" meant that the queen's feudal right of escheatment upon the death of each owner was not applicable. Heirs would come into their estates, with whatever encumbrances, by right, and not by the monarch's discretion.

Beginning with the Virginia charter of 1606 the words *fee simple* no longer appear in the patents of the colonies. Instead the property right, the tenure of the property, is described as free and common socage. Since land held in that tenure was also heritable and could be sold freely and devised by will, the two tenures could be easily confused, and were. The confusion continued to befog legal discussion of American land titles into the nineteenth century, when it was argued that even if the land was owned in fee simple, the tenure of it was free and common socage. There were reasons to make this distinction, rooted in the practices of English feudalism, and the words remained after the reality had utterly disappeared. It was this form of English land tenure, free and common socage, that was used to organize and settle colonial America. From the beginning until the American Revolution, the

[3] Thorpe, *Federal and State Constitutions,* p. 54.

[4] Susan Myra Kingsbury, ed., *The Records of the Virginia Company of London: The Court Book* (Washington, D.C., 1906), p. 12.

American land, the ultimate ownership of it, belonged to the English monarch, to grant as he, or she, pleased. Private titles in the hands of people like ordinary farmers devolved from this source.

In the law of England only the king had absolute property right (after William the Conqueror simplified his property right problems). Technically, all landholders were tenants of the king; all land was held as a tenement, even land held in fee simple, that is, as an estate of inheritance.[5] This principle was the basic root of English feudalism, whose object in land distribution was the maintenance and control of a military caste. There was a vast array of property rights in the feudal tenures, but by the seventeenth century many of them had become obsolete, and only the skeleton remained (see chapter 5). The skeleton is what came, in particular ways, as property right with the English colonists. Basically it was still feudal. Its legitimacy still rested on the legitimacy of the crown. There was no other route to property title. As Blackstone put it, writing in his *Commentaries:* "Thus all the land in the kingdom is supposed to be holden, mediately or immediately, of the king, who, is styled the lord *Paramount,* or above all. . . . In this manner are all the lands of the kingdom holden, which are in the hands of subjects, for, according to Sir Edward Coke, in the law of England we have not properly allodium."[6] And in such manner were all lands in English America held, at least theoretically (colonial attitudes about quitrents indicated that it had become theoretical indeed across the ocean by the eighteenth century).

During the two centuries after it was transplanted to America, free and common socage tenure naturally underwent some modifications, both by local custom and by the exercise of some quirks from ancient English tenure law. When, in the late 1780s, it came time for the new nation to establish a land policy for its public lands west of the Appalachians, the congressmen chose from among these developments and came up with what was perhaps the most revolutionary creation of the period. The Northwest Ordinance of 1787 discarded many of the complexities of the

[5] Blackstone, bk. 2, p. 47; see also W. A. Maitland, *The Constitutional History of England* (Cambridge, 1961), pp. 24-25, and Marshall Harris, *The Origin of the Land Tenure System in the United States* (Ames, Iowa, 1953), pp. 4-5.

[6] Bk. 2, p. 47.

common English law of real property. It allowed property to be freely devised by will and specified convenient methods of conveying land to a new purchaser. It broadened the line of descent for estates of persons dying intestate.[7] Essentially, once the national government had made the initial sale of a parcel of land, it stepped out of the picture. There were still barriers to absolute ownership: taxes must be paid; land could be given in judgement against private debt and taken in eminent domain proceedings, but these potential encumbrances were owed to the immediate local governments, which were in the hands of the people. Generally, a man could buy the land he wanted, sell what he wanted, and grant it by will, in what parts and pieces he pleased. Land had become a commodity and a productive resource privately owned and controlled, a basic part of the system known to the world as American capitalism.

This capitalism, logically, required such a development, since perfect adjustment to changes in productive techniques could not occur if some necessary factors of production were institutionally withheld from the market. Similarly, perfect divisibility (or the more divisible the better) among the prime factors of production, land, the labor force, and the instruments of capital was best achieved if the relevant agents of production could be apportioned with minimum friction according to the demands of technology and the market. For decades, this feature of American property right was instrumental in determining the acquisition of farms and ranches, mining properties, land grants from the government, and rights of squatter preemption, as the frontier cut its way across the continent and the land was taken up. It created great problems, was probably not a just way of doing things, but as the eminent American economic historian Lance Davis once said, "it was simple and fast."

The system had come a long way from its origins. By force of arms the power of the people had replaced that of the crown in the new republic. Hence it was understandable, years later, in 1830, when Robert Dane of Massachusetts boasted to Daniel

---

[7]*Documents Illustrative of the Formation of the Union,* "Ordinance of 1787, July 13, 1787," sec. 2, pp. 47-48.

Webster of his role in these great innovations—especially legitimacy of ownership without benefit of the crown. Much else was
swept away: the English common law of descent, together with
the Mosaic system of New England, Pennsylvania, and elsewhere,
the right of the double portion to the eldest son. "When I mention
the formation of this Ordinance, it is proper to explain. It consists
of three parts. Ist, the titles to estates, real and personal, by deed,
by will, and by descent; also personal, by delivery. These titles
occupy the first part of the Ordinance . . . it omits the double
share to the oldest son. These titles were made to take root in the
first and early settlements, in 400,000 square miles. Such titles so
taking root, we well know, are, in their nature, in no small degree
permanent; so, vastly important. I believe these were the first
titles to property, completely republican, in Federal America;
being in no part whatever feudal or monarchical."[8] But these
innovations were not totally new: "I mention the Ordinance of
'87 was framed, mainly, from the laws of Massachusetts . . . meaning the titles to estates."[9] By thus relying on colonial experience,
history was made to pay off for the Republic, and what had
proved good was used, with no thought of reverting to the original
English model.

This result, the determination of the nature of property right in
real estate, and the power to control its evolution toward the
modern American fee simple, was one of the greatest achievements
of the nonmarket social control in the colonial period. By the end
of the eighteenth century the right of ownership of the American
land up to the edges of the old Northwest, wrested from the
aboriginal tribes by right of the lord paramount of the English
nation, was typically found in the family farm. When one considers the infinity of alternatives, it would be difficult, in the
abstract, to think of a more unlikely result. Yet the alternatives
were not available to those who lived by English law, and that law
further restricted those in America to only one path, socage. Since
socage was not a military tenure, for example, the incidents of

    [8]Albert Bushnell Hart, ed., *American History Told by Contemporaries* (New York,
1901), 3:155.
    [9]Ibid., p. 157.

chivalry could not evolve from it—it could only produce more freedom, not less. The law in England was in fact moving in the same direction simultaneously; feudalism's military tenures were abolished in England in 1660 during the reign of Charles II.[10] After that, free and common socage was also the sole tenure of real property in England, except for certain minor tenures which survived.

This parallelism poses an interesting question for the pure theorist of institutional development. If the nature of the property right in land is believed to represent the outcome of rational economic forces—for example, the conservation of the scarce factor by free substitution of the more abundant factors—what evidence is there that the crude ratios of land to labor in England and in the American colonies were sufficiently similar to explain the emergence in both places of free and common socage land tenures at roughly the same time? To understand this one needs some help from the facts. The socage tenure was not developed in the colonies but was established there arbitrarily by the crown in the colonial charters—by the king's "merest motion," as the charters express it. Whatever forces moved the evolution of real property rights in England toward this simple tenure also settled that form of tenure in Amerca. English, not American, conditions created the American tenure. After its arrival in America, socage tenure slowly lost the known duties and extra fees, ground rents, and oaths of fealty and evolved toward the simple tenures of the Northwest Ordinance. The English tenure maintains such curiosities as reserved ground rents to this day. So the evolution was not by equal degrees in the two countries, after all, and it may be argued that the continuously simplified tenures in America represented the market's recognition that greater freedom was due to the cultivator of the land in order to conserve his labor than was true in England as the years passed. One can grant that much to pure theory in this matter. But the establishment of the tenure of free and common socage, the one that became our form of land ownership, was due to an outside force. American history alone

[10]12 Charles II, c. 24 (1660).

will not provide this information, nor will any amount of theorizing. In any case, the theorist, if he eschewed "historical inertia" as a causal element, would still need to explain the continuation of feudal services combined with leases and fees simple in New York State until the mid-nineteenth century, a phenomenon we will examine in due course.

4
Limitation of Indian Property Rights

John Marshall has made his decision. Now let him enforce it.
Andrew Jackson on *Worcester* v. *Georgia* decision

Discussion of American property rights in real estate must involve the American Indians, for the question of the legitimacy of land titles in general in the colonies is inextricably mixed up with the elimination of the Indians from their lands, from the start. Queen Elizabeth, for example, while warranting Raleigh's activities to "discover, search, find out, and view such remote heathen and barbarous lands, countries, and territories, not actually possessed of any Christian Prince, nor inhabited by Christian People . . . to have, holde, occupy and enjoy,"[1] and promising to make restitution to any such Christian princes disturbed by these adventurers, did not provide for the heathen rulers. Nor did the charters granted by her successors, apart from occasional platitudes. The Indian titles did not exist, except for the right of occupancy, which proved to be not far from that of a tenant-at-will. Treaties, purchases, and wars in the following two centuries did not really resolve the problem, nor is it resolved completely to this day. Thus when the issue came before the Supreme Court in a complex land case which was the first test of the contract clause of the Constitution, *Fletcher* v. *Peck*, the quizzical tone of Marshall's decision is readily understood. "The majority of the court is of opinion that the nature of the Indian title, which is certainly to be respected by all courts, until it be legitimately extinguished, is not such as to be absolutely repugnant to seisin in fee on the part of the state."[2] *Seisin in fee*, as used here, is a feudal term for absolute title, and tragedies like the Cherokee removal were to show what the new

[1] Thorpe, *Federal and State Constitutions*, p. 53.
[2] 6 Cranch 142-43 (February term, 1810).

republic thought was legitimate extinguishment.[3] Indian title, where respected by the colonists, had somehow to be derived from the same source of legitimacy as their own titles, the crown or its successor, the United States. Herein lay one of the great tragedies of this history, and it began with right of conquest.

Discussion of Indian rights to real property can be handled in a short chapter indeed. The comment by President Jackson on Chief Justice Marshall's decision in *Worcester* v. *Georgia* in 1834 about sums it up.[4] The people of Georgia were going to take the lands of the Cherokee Nation, and the Cherokees were going to have to take the long trail across the Mississippi. Since the entire development of the United States from the beginning was predicated upon occupation of a continent which also was inhabited by another race, Indian property rights were tenuous in the eyes of the growing European population.

The letters patent of 1492 from Queen Isabella and King Ferdinand to Columbus are essentially a license for conquest and plunder, to be practiced upon "some islands and a continent in the ocean"[5] that he proposed to visit. The crowned heads of England were not innovators in this regard. It was part of the European tradition that Christians had a natural right to conquest and dominion in the non-Christian world, from pole to pole in all directions, and this settled tradition produced "concrete historical problems" which still disrupt international relations. It would be pointless to speculate upon the sources of this cultural chauvinism. In American history it simply meant that the English crown granted land, to white men and others, from the red man's patrimony and from the lands of the original French, Spanish, Dutch, Swedish and Portuguese settlers as the opportunity arose. The

[3]Kent, *Commentaries,* 3:508. Jackson, in his message to Congress on Feb. 15, 1832, said that all Indians should be removed to lands west of the Mississippi (*Messages and Papers of the Presidents,* ed. James D. Richardson [Washington, D.C., 1902], 565-66). Congress had already legislated to that effect in 1830, and did so again promptly on July 14, 1832.

[4]Samuel Eliot Morison and Henry Steele Commager, *The Growth of the American Republic* (New York, 1942), 1: 489.

[5]Thorpe, pp. 39-40.

other Europeans, from the Spanish to the Russians, held essentially the same views of the right of conquest.

In his *Commentaries on American Law,* the great jurist Chancellor James Kent, of New York, writing in 1826, produced long, learned, brilliant, and tortuous pages on this subject, but he could come to no conclusions except, essentially, that reality was justified by the facts. Some of his language is worth our consideration. "Each nation claimed the right to regulate for itself, in exclusion of all others, the relation which was to subsist between the discoverer and the Indians. That relation necessarily impaired, to a considerable degree, the rights of the original inhabitants, and an ascendency was asserted in consequence of the superior genius of the Europeans, founded on civilization and Christianity, and their superiority in the means and in the art of war."[6] Or, "The settlement of that part of America now composing the United States has been attended with as little violence and aggression, on the part of the whites . . . as is compatible with the fact of the entry of a race of civilized men into the territory of savages."[7] These passages were written before most of the Sioux had even seen a white man and, being high legal authority, boded ill for them. So did the notion that land belonged by right to cultivators of it: "if unsettled and sparcely scattered tribes of hunters and fishermen show no disposition or capacity to emerge from the savage to the agricultural and civilized state of man, their right to keep the fairest portions of the earth a mere wilderness, filled with wild beasts, for the sake of hunting, becomes utterly inconsistent with the civilization and moral improvement of mankind."[8]

But now let us go backward in time nearly two centuries, to the great Puritan leader John Winthrop, who held the same views and claimed, naturally, a biblical justification, set forth in the *General Considerations for the Plantation in New England,* usually attributed to Winthrop and circulated in England by the Puritans before their embarkation for Massachusetts Bay. After stating that "the whole earth is the Lord's garden and hee hath given it to the sons of Adam to bee tilled and improved by them," the essay turns to

---

[6]Kent, 3:505; see also Harris, *Origin of Land Tenure System in U.S.,* pp. 62-68.
[7]Kent, 3:516.
[8]Ibid., p. 514.

"objections" and answers to them. "By what warrant have we to take that land which is and hath been of long time possessed by others of the sons of Adam?" The answer is worth considering at length.

That which is common to all is proper to none. This savage people ruleth over many lands without title or property; for they inclose no ground, neither have they cattell to maintagne it, but remove their dwellings as they have occasion, or as they can prevail against their neighbors. And why may not Christians have liberty to go and dwell amongst them in their waste lands and woods (leaving them such places as they have manured for their corne) as lawfully as Abraham did among the Sodomites? For God hathe given to the sons of man a twofold right to the earth; there is a naturall right and a civil right. The first right was naturall when men held the earth in common, every man sowing and feeding where he pleased: Then, as men and cattell increased, they appropriated some parcells of ground by enclosing and peculiar manur-ance, and this in tyme got them a civil right. Such was the right which Ephron the Hittite had to the field of Machpelah, wherein Abraham could not bury a dead corpse without leave, though for the out parts of the countrey which lay common, he dwelt upon them and tooke the fruite of them at his pleasure. . . . There is more than enough for them and us. . . . God hath consumed the natives with a miraculous plague, whereby the greater part of the country is left voide of inhabitants. . . . We shall come in with good leave of the natives."[9]

The last information, the plague and the possibility of peace with the Indians, had come primarily from the experience of the Plymouth colonists. The miraculous plague was also noted years later by Cotton Mather: "Another thing that give them no little Exercise, was the *Fear of the Indians,* by whom they were some-times Alarm'd. But this fear was wonderfully prevented, not only by *Intestine Wars* happening then to fall out among those *Bar-barians,* but chiefly by the *Small-Pox,* which prov'd a *great Plague* unto them, and particularly to one of the Princes in the

---

[9]Thomas Hutchinson, *The Hutchinson Papers* (Albany, 1865), 1:30, 33-34; see also, p. 156, a report of 1645 of the Commissioners of the United Colonies treating the recent obliteration of the "Narowgansett" Indians, who had violated their agreements by harboring survivors of the Pequods and by moving onto Pequod land "which by right of conquest, appertaines to the English."

Massachusetts-Bay, who yet seemed hopefully to be Christioniz'd before he Dy'd."[10]

It is the case that the people of Massachusetts generally did buy, or try to buy, their land from Indian chiefs. Individuals were forbidden to buy directly from the Indians; the crown or its representatives had to serve as intermediaries. The same was generally true in the other colonies. Cotton Mather considered land purchase in Massachusetts from the Indians "an instance of the most imaginable civility . . . since the great patent for 'New England in America' gave the Plymouth Company all the lands . . . from sea to sea, provided the same be not actually possessed or inhabited by any other Christian Prince or state."[11] But war and conquest played their parts too. It was a complex, difficult, and bloody history, with the Indians at the continuous disadvantage, since they had no title to their land except right of occupancy where convenient to the settlers. At the end of the nineteenth century Theodore Roosevelt wrote of the problem: "To recognize the Indian ownership of the limitless prairies and forests of this continent—that is, to consider the dozen squalid savages who hunted at long intervals over a territory of a thousand square miles as owning it outright—necessarily implies a similar recognition of the claims of every white hunter, squatter, horsethief, or wandering cattle-man."[12] To the "Rough Rider" the solution was simple: "With the best of intentions, it was wholly impossible for any government to evolve order out of such a chaos without resort to the ultimate arbitrator—the sword."[13]

So from beginning to end primary title was deemed to come by right of conquest, Indian title being inferior in the views of the crown, the settlers, the United States government, the Supreme Court, and Theodore Roosevelt. People like Roger Williams who argued against this view were not thanked for their logic.[14] As a

---

[10]*Magnalia Christi Americana* (London, 1702), bk. 1, p. 22.

[11]Ibid., p. 72; see also Kent, 3:514-15; Harris, pp. 155-78.

[12]Theodore Roosevelt, *The Winning of the West* (New York, 1889), 1:331.

[13]Ibid., p. 333; see also Harris, pp. 62-65, on right of conquest.

[14]George Bancroft, *History of the Colonization of the United States,* 21st ed. (Boston, 1866), 1:369.

legal and historical matter, then, any notion of an absolute Indian title may be laid aside.

We come then to the absolute title, that of England's king, and his rights and powers to distribute titles to lands for his own purposes. From these titles came our own form of property in real estate. Indian titles could only come to whites, legitimately, through the crown or, later, the various government agencies of the United States.

5

The American Tenure
and Its Establishment

Considering what colonization was, the movement of a large population over the ocean to a new country, the English colonization was remarkably disciplined. It is true that the Americans, in the end, chafed under that discipline. But the discipline was real, the control provided, while it was necessary, a framework of rules which kept chaos at bay. It is a misunderstanding of American history to suppose that the colonists came over the ocean and created the new country entirely out of their native genius. Just as the old Northwest was settled under the Ordinances of 1785 and 1787, and the new West under the laws of the United States, so the colonial world took form under English law. The Americans changed some of the rules and in the end revolted. But except for frontier squatters, they did not live outside their laws. The colonies were part of the larger English society until the Revolution, and the social controls of that society prevailed until they were overthrown and new rules were provided by American governments.

In colonial America land granted by the crown generally conveyed two fundamental sets of social constraints. First, the specific English tenure of free and common socage was granted the owners of land; and second, the colonists who settled those lands were, in addition, guaranteed the rights, privileges, and immunities which were enjoyed by natural English subjects. The latifundia of Spanish America, great estates populated by peasants with uncertain property rights, were not possible in English America. The socage tenure gradually evolved toward the standard American tenure, and the guarantee of English law, it has been argued, was a major contributor to those forces which led to the American Revolution. The colonists believed that taxes laid upon them from London, and not through the colonial assemblies, were usurpations of a privilege jealously guarded in England. The people should tax themselves through their own agencies. Property rights and taxing powers were linked, since the ultimate source of taxation in colonial America was the land itself, and under socage tenure, land was free from all except fixed exactions.[1]

It is far beyond the scope of this book to study fully the evolution of the English land tenure system.[2] But our own system derives from English feudalism both in word and form and cannot be understood without a brief excursion into English feudal land law. Here we need only to concentrate upon those basic parts that evolved into our own system of landowning. We need to examine (1) the grant of title and (2) the rights of alienation and devise. In these aspects of the English system we find the permutations of our analytical variables in chapter 1: number, entry, price, and quality.

We need to theorize a bit. To understand English feudal land law one should consider property rights to be divisible into many parts. Any piece of land could support many kinds of rights which had economic value and could be exchanged for obligations, which might be services, payments in kind, or money. (Consider the rights to water, timber, minerals, easements—to sell any, or all, or to rent or lease, them—still associated with a given piece of land. In feudal England the rights of owners of real property—and hence the obligations of those who acquired land—were far more extensive in number.) The entire piece of property may then be seen as a bundle of rights. The total bundle of such rights in England was owned outright by the king, after William the Conqueror. Any claim by a person to any part of that bundle could only be legitimate if the king (or his agents) had granted that part, either directly or to another party who had the authority to grant that right or to sell it to someone else. English feudalism in land is thus often referred to as a ladder, with a system of property rights (and appropriate titles belonging to the holders) descending from the

[1]See Blackstone, *Commentaries,* bk. 2, pp. 48, 60-62, 77-78, on socage; also, Sir William Holdsworth, *A History of English Law,* 4th ed. (London, 1936), 2:348, 3:51-54; Maitland, *Constitutional History of England,* pp. 31-32, 35.

[2]See Blackstone, bk. 2, on English tenures generally; Holdsworth, 3:29-275, on English tenures and land law; Maitland, pp. 23-29; S. F. C. Milson, *Historical Foundations of the Common Law* (London, 1969), pp. 88-205. Application of these tenures to America is the subject of Harris, *Origins of Land Tenure System in U.S.*

king to the lowliest peasant, each owner of each part of the bundle paying the person above him in services, goods, or money, for whatever rights he enjoyed. No one could legitimately sell more parts of the total property rights bundle than he had to begin with, just as one might not dispose of his neighbor's land itself.

The king's grants of property rights in land were given in return for services, rents, and fees he was to receive. The king, as lord paramount, was free to set the conditions he chose—constrained after 1215 by Magna Carta. The major services the king wanted were military and, to a lesser degree, religious. Since all property rights in land devolved from the king, all owners of property in land were technically his tenants. Those at the top of the feudal ladder who received their grants of land directly from the king were his tenants in chief, and their grants were called tenures in capite. The king's grants were contracts, stating the nature of the agreements (the amount of rights from the total bundle that had been granted), the payment or consideration involved, and the conditions to be fulfilled to complete the agreements.

In theory all the feudal property rights derived from military, or chivalrous, tenures reverted, or escheated, to the king upon the death of each of his chief tenants. The king was then to find a new tenant who could fulfill the terms of the property right contract in question. Similarly, death among the lower classes of the tenants of property was occasion for their property rights to escheat to their lords. When, in the thirteenth century, the descendants of military tenants gained the right to inherit directly without escheatment (upon payment of a fee, the relief, only), the fee simple of medieval England was born. Whenever lower classes owned land that descended by direct inheritance only upon payment of a relief, and did not escheat, the tenure was a form of socage. Thus, these two tenures were both estates of direct inheritance, even though one grew out of Norman feudalism and the other was descended from the Saxons. In time the names of the two tenures would become interchangeable. After 1660, when most military tenures were abolished, free and common socage remained, and it came to be called fee simple. This has been a source of great confusion because lands in American were not lands granted for military services, yet the tenures were called fee simple. They were actually socage tenures, whatever the colonists called them.

From this simple set of elements arose the complexities of England's land law. Land has to be worked to yield its fruits, and since man is mortal, ways had to be found to pass the rights and obligations of property from one generation to the next. Owners of rights in great estates could subdivide their rights among others in return for suitable payments from these tenants of their own, just as the king had done. Only fee simple lands and socage lands could be sold outright, aliened to a buyer or grantee and his heirs, so care had to be taken that the successive subdivisions of land from one generation to the next did not reduce the king's own power—his rights. The successive subdivision, or subinfeudation, of the land quite early began to create a network of obligations between lords and their own tenants which, by extenuation, weakened the king's own powers, and in 1290, in the statute *Quia emptores,* the further subversion of the central power by subinfeudation was forbidden.[3] After *Quia emptores* tenants who had alienable property rights could freely dispose of those rights, but if they did, they stepped out of the feudal ladder, and the buyer stepped in in their stead, with the same obligations to the king or his lords as the seller previously had. As the great English historian F. W. Maitland put it, "no new rungs could be put into the feudal ladder."[4] The structure was frozen. One who acquired given property rights could not then create a new little feudal system among his own tenants. He could lease, rent, or sell the rights of all or any part of his property. But no new feudal property rights could be created beyond those acquired.

Quia emptores was suspended in the charters of some colonies, Maryland, Delaware, and in Pennsylvania (to one degree only), creating the possibility of subinfeudation there. The proprietors in Maryland and Delaware and their tenants could create manors in a feudal chain; William Penn could create manors, but those who held those manors could not, in turn, create more. Nothing lasting

[3] 18 Edward I, c. 1; Blackstone, p. 79 n.(30); Holdsworth, 2:348; Kent, *Commentaries,* 4:474; Milson, pp. 97-102.

[4] P. 32.

came of American feudalism in these three colonies. But something very lasting indeed came from *Quia emptores.* What it did for the Englishman and, later on, the American colonist (and even later, us) was guarantee that the purchaser of rights in real property got all the rights sold to him and acquired no more obligations with the property than he had agreed to assume. The statute of Edward I thus still guarantees the clean entry and exit of modern American owners of real property when those property rights change hands by purchase.

The military tenants of the king were the main props of the feudal system. But even though they could lease and sell their lands and acquire tenants of their own (within the bounds set by *Quia emptores*), in England ultimate loyalty was due only to the king himself,[5] which made the English crown a central authority in a way that Continental feudalism, with extensive subinfeudation, could never achieve. In time property rights in England granted by the king or the chief tenants came to be granted for economic terms, most commonly for payment of rents and services. Since some rights could be reserved, all need not be sold, even lands aliened could carry an obligatory reserved ground rent to be paid in perpetuity to the chief tenant, no matter how many hands the land passed through. The idea of this rent was that it left the buyer "quit and free" of other duties, payments, and obligations. Such simplified obligations were the quitrents of colonial America.

The catalogue of feudal payments and obligations is fairly staggering. If the tenants were villeins, or serfs, and could not leave the land, they were bound to the land. Their services usually varied with conditions, were not fixed, and were for life only. When tenants died, their land theoretically fell back upon their lords, and new arrangements were made with the next tenants. The payment of a relief for inherited land or an entry fine for purchased land were formalities which placed the new tenant, heir, or purchaser into the system. For a serf bound to the land to succeed his father a tax (the heriot, usually the best cow or other beast) still had to be paid over to the lord of the manor. New

---

[5] Ibid.

tenants could not take over, or enter, the land until the new agreement was made. Because most men were illiterate, a formal witnessed ceremony was required for property rights in real estate to change hands. With a little ceremony, sometimes cutting and handing over a twig or digging up and handing over a piece of sod in the presence of the immediate neighbors, entry was made.[6] This was called seisin in livery, and until the *Statute of Frauds* (1677) was the only transfer of land recognized by common law. To this day, in legal jargon in this country, to be seised of land is to have proper title to it. Whatever else feudalism was, it was personal; the relationships were human, in the modern parlance.

One of the feudal property rights an ordinary person might acquire was that of free and common socage. Its English origins are shadowy, except all agree that it antedates the Norman conquest. It was a desirable property right for several reasons. The king granted land in socage, and socage lands could be acquired by direct purchase and owned in perpetuity. As we have noted, socage tenure shared the characteristic of direct heritability with the fee simple of some of the military tenures. But socage was no military tenure, and so it did not carry the load of incidents of chivalry. Socage tenures carried only fixed and certain obligations. Once agreed to, the terms could not be changed at will or because of other irregular needs of feudal overlords such as to finance marriages. The terms of socage tenures could include such burdens as perpetual ground rents reserved by the seller, reliefs upon inheritance, and entry fines upon purchase. Some socage tenures were base—carried the obligation to perform manual labor—but this villein socage is to be distinguished from free and common socage.[7] Military service could not be required of the socman, and most important in that uncertain world, the seller (donor) of

---

[6]Kent, 4:529-37. With such a ceremony William Penn entered his fief in Pennsylvania on Aug. 27, 1682 (Edward Channing, *A History of the United States* [New York, 1924], 2:112). The freemen of Malmesbury, according to legend, received 500 acres of common land from King Athelstan after the Battle of Brunanburh in 937. Entry is still made by succeeding generations of Malmesbury men accompanied by the recital of "Turf and twig I give to thee, as King Athelstan gave to me."

[7]Blackstone, bk. 2, pp. 77-78. The idea of a single tenure of socage is misleading; see Douglass North and Robert Thomas, *The Rise of the Western World* (Cambridge, 1973), p. 35.

socage land held no right of wardship. If the socager, or socman, died and left a minor heir, the land did not escheat; instead the next of kin (who could not inherit) became the guardian. The guardian had no right of waste during the years of the heir's minority and was accountable to the heir for the yield of the property. When the heir reached fourteen, the guardian handed over the estate to him. This was a tenure of simplicity compared to other feudal tenures. In fact, it could obviously exist without any feudal lord at all, so long as there was someone—the king, a colonial government, or later, a state—to whom the certain and fixed payment could be made to validate title. Socage was as much a part of the feudal system as knight service, copyhold, petit and grand serjeanty, frankelmoign, or the other tenures of the time. Yet in a fundamental sense it was different, for it could exist logically without feudal society to give it meaning. And indeed, as Marshall Harris has shown, the feudal aids became first the quit-rents of colonial America and then our modern property taxes.[8] Fines for alienation became our stamp taxes on deeds, together with state recording and registration fees. Escheatment still exists by the same name, except that the state government fills the role of feudal lord. Stripped of all but a single initial payment, free and common socage could be land ownership by simple purchase, the fee simple absolute, as it became known in the United States.

Free and common socage tenure thus developed into an important facet of the feudal system. It was, or could be, a commercialized tenure, making land alienable by simple purchase; because its holders were not bound to the land (were not villeins), they were liable for known obligations which could be capitalized, thus putting a firm price on the land. Already alienable and inheritable, free and common socage officially became devisable by will in 1540 under Henry VIII's Statute of Wills. With that act, holders

[8]For the correspondence of our modern practice with English feudal procedures, see Harris, p. 410. Holdsworth, in discussing the evolution of tenures and land law, remarks of the fixed payment, usually in money, characteristic of the socage tenure: "With the increase in the tendency of the land law to become simply property law it is the money rent characteristic of socage tenure which becomes the most valuable service" (2:348). He also says, "It was the least encumbered of all the tenures with obsolete and oppressive incidents, reminiscent of an older day when land-holding involved public rights and duties as well as private rights of ownership" (3:53).

of socage tenure of all sorts, so long as it was not held directly by knight service (among the last remnants of military tenures), could "have full and free liberty, power and authority to give, dispose, will and devise, as well by his last will and testament in writing, or by any act or acts lawfully executed in his life."[9]

As a potential article of commerce the socage tenure was thus perfected. In fact, so powerful was its influence in England that by 1660, as we have seen, in the reign of Charles II, all military tenures were swept away in a single act of Parliament and were converted to free and common socage. England was moving toward a commercial society and away from the last vestiges of feudalism. Its colonies overseas had the advantage of having had no military feudalism in the form of land tenure; fortunately, only free and common socage was brought to America.

From the Virginia Charter of 1606 onward, the contracts, or letters patent granted by English monarchs to American settlers, were very similar in their essentials. The crown granted lands to a company, like the Virginia Company, or to a person, like William Bradford, Lord Baltimore, or William Penn. The place of the contract is stated, a royal residence, say Windsor Castle or Greenwich Manor; the consideration is stated, usually something symbolic like the "two Beaver Skins, to bee delivered at Our said Castle of Windsor on the First Day of January of every Year" which William Penn was obliged to pay or the "Two Indian Arrows of these Parts" to be delivered at Windsor "every Year on Tuesday of Easter Week" that was demanded of Lord Baltimore and his heirs, and the reservation of the royal fifth of any gold and silver ore. The contracts specified heirs of both parties so that it could not be conceived of as a life tenancy. Then the obligations to be performed, the terms of settlement, were laid out. This document became not only the contract between the king and the company or proprietor involved but the constitution of the colony itself.

It was through these charters, technically, that the heritage of England was transferred to the New World. But the laws of colonial Massachusetts indicate that apart from the direct infusion of

[9] 32 Henry VIII, c. 1., art. 1, "The Act of wills, wards, primer seisins, whereby a man may devise two parts of his land."

the Old Testament, the English colonists, at first, might not have produced domestic government too different from that of England even without the benefit of the charters. The colonists did what they knew how to do. The charters were very specific. The Virginia charter of 1606 was granted by James I to two companies, to the City of London Company, called the First Company, and to persons from Bristol, Exeter, and Plymouth, called the Second Company. Their structures, powers, and privileges were carefully specified. They were to enjoy a monopoly on the lands specified which were to be held "in free and common Soccage only, and not in Capite."[10] The lands were to be divided "in such Manner and Form, and for such estates, as shall be set down by the council of the said Colony, or the most part of them respectively." The rights of the settlers were protected: "all and every the Persons being our Subjects, which shall dwell and inhabit within . . . the said Colonies and Plantations, and every of their children, which shall happen to be born . . . shall HAVE and enjoy all Liberties, Franchises, and Immunities . . . as if they had been abiding and born, within this our Realm of England." Elizabeth, in her patent to Raleigh, had said that the prospective colonists "shall and may have all the privledges of free Denizens, and persons native of England, and within our allegiance . . . as if they were borne and personally resident within our said Realme of England."[11]

Similarly the 1620 charter for "New England in America," granted to Sir Ferdinando Gorges and his associates, gave corporate powers to their company and allowed them to pass necessary laws "so always as the same be not contrary to the Laws and Statutes of this our Realme of England." The land was "to be holden to us, our Heires, and Successors, as of our Manor of East-Greenwich, in our County of Kent, in free and comon Soccage and not in . . . Capite, nor by Knight's Service, yielding and paying therefore to Us, . . . the fifth part, of the Ores of Gold and Silver." The charter of Massachusetts, in 1629, granted the land in socage for payment of the royal fifth and allowed the people to acquire

---

[10] Thorpe, *Federal and State Constitutions*, p. 3789.

[11] Thorpe, pp. 3789, 3788, 54.

and dispose of their lands "as other our liege People of this our Realme of England." The people were to have rights "as if they and everie of them were borne within the Realme of England."[12]

Connecticut, which was originally settled in two colonies, at Hartford and New Haven, was singular. Hartford, a Plymouth Colony trading post, was preempted by settlers from Massachusetts. New Haven was organized in a remarkable demonstration of grassroots constitution making in 1638-39, without leave of the crown. After the English Civil War, in 1662, Charles II gave Connecticut a royal charter. The land was held in free and common socage, and the people had "all Liberties and Immunities . . . as if they and every of them were born within the realm of *England*."[13] It is worth noting that when James II tried to consolidate all the northern colonies in 1686, in the "Commission of Sir Edward Andros for the Dominion of New England," a venture commonly held to have been despotic, the royal rein was kept on to some extent. Even the laws of Andros were required to be "as consonant and agreeable to the laws and statutes of this our realm of England as the present state and condition of our subjects . . . will admit."[14] In 1664, when James was merely the duke of York and his brother Charles II set him up as a proprietor in the New World, the grant had been for free and common socage tenure and the originality of lawmaking had been limited "as neare as conveniently may be agreeable to the laws statutes and government of this our realme of England."[15]

In the proprietary colony of Maryland, granted in 1632, Charles I created an astonishing anachronism, a government modeled after County Durham, the ancient county palatine ruled by the bishop of Durham that was set up by William the Conqueror on the model of the frontier mark of Charlemagne. Thus the Maryland charter gives the impression that in the person of Cecilius Calvert, Baron Baltimore, Charles I had taken on a partner, and it was in truth meant to be a kingdom within a kingdom. Lord Baltimore and his heirs were to have all the rights of "any Bishop of Durham, within the bishopric or county palatine of Durham, in our kingdom of England."[16]

---

[12]Ibid., pp. 1832, 1852, 1856-57.   [13]Ibid., p. 533.   [14]Ibid., p. 1863.
[15]Ibid., p. 1638.   [16]Ibid., p. 1678.

The statute *Quia emptores* was set aside in Maryland, and so subinfeudation was allowed. The chief tenant, Lord Baltimore, was empowered to set up baronies and manors and to establish feudal manor courts—courts baron and courts leet, or view of frankpledge, a form of court for petty offenses whose origin seems to have been group responsibility for individual crimes.[17] Since Lord Baltimore was creating a new nobility in his domain, because *Quia emptores* was lifted, he was exercising a power that only the king of England exercised at home. Lands were escheated back to the lord proprietor, not the crown, and quitrents and other payments due from landholding were recorded on rent rolls, to be paid to the proprietor, Lord Baltimore.

The land given to Lord Baltimore, being "partly occupied by savages having no knowledge of the Divine Being," was granted to him in free and common socage, "by fealty only for all services, and not in capite, nor by Knight's Service," in return for three arrowheads and the royal fifth of precious metals.[18] The proprietor, however, could grant land under whatever conditions he wished; there is surviving evidence of at least two reliefs paid for entry to socage land at courts baron held in Maryland: at St. Clement's Manor, in 1672, "We present that upon the death of Mr. Robert Sly there is a Reliefe due to the Lord and that Mr. Gerald Sly is his next heire who hath sworn fealty accordingly";[19] and one for a land sale, with no date given: "We present an alienation from James Edmonds to Thomas Oakley upon which there is a relief due to the lord, and Oakley hath sworn fealty."[20]

The lord proprietor was abjured to act with the "Advice, Assent and Approbation of the Free-Men," the laws to be "not repugnant or contrary . . ."[21] The settlers, despite the power of Lord

---

[17]Ibid., p. 1685. *Quia emptores* was later reimposed in Maryland (Harris, p. 396). The absence of manor courts in New England bemused Sumner Power (*Puritan Village*, pp. 11, 142), but there could be no new manors created in the New World where *Quia emptores* was not lifted, and it was not in New England.

[18]Thorpe, pp. 1677, 1679.

[19]Richard B. Morris, "Primogeniture and Entailed Estates in America," *Columbia Law Review* 27 (1927): 25.

[20]Newton B. Mereness, *Maryland as a Proprietary Province* (New York, 1920), pp. 408-10.

[21]Thorpe, pp. 1679, 1680.

Baltimore, were given by his Gracious Majesty the rights of "Natives and Liege-Men of Us . . . of our Kingdom of England and Ireland," and they were to be free to use their lands, "to inherit, or otherwise purchase, receive, take, have, hold, buy, and posses, . . . and the same to give, sell, alien, and bequeath; and likewise all Privileges, Franchises and Liberties of this our Kingdom of England . . . in the same manner as our Liege-Men born, or to be borne without our said Kingdom of England."[22]

To be sure, the lord proprietor had extensive powers delegated to him, including even, as captain general of the province, the powers to raise armies, wage war, and even, explicitly, to "put to death the captives"[23] —the Stuart touch. Even so, the general rules of tenure, free socage, and rights of Englishmen prevailed within this Lilliputian monarchy in the wilderness. The Pennsylvania charter was similar to Maryland's in granting socage and guaranteeing English rights, but in Pennsylvania the guarantee was supererogatory because Penn's own governmental instruments for his colony were far in advance of the English constitution of the day.[24]

Socage tenure and common English rights prevailed in the other colonies too, except the last, Georgia. In the 1732 charter of this colony, designed to relieve honest debtors, the consideration taken for the grant was not so lighthearted as the beaver skins and arrowheads of earlier times. It specified that the land was "to be holden of us, in our County of Middlesex, in free and common socage, and not in capite; yielding and paying to us, our heirs and successors, forever, the sum of four shillings for every hundred acres of the said lands which the said corporation shall grant, demise, plant, or settle."[25] By then it was seen that the mainland colonies

---

[22]Ibid., p. 1681. [23]Ibid, p. 1682.

[24]I will not discuss Pennsylvania's charter more than minimally here. I have treated it elsewhere at some length: Jonathan Hughes, *The Vital Few* (Boston, 1966; rept. New York, 1973), pp. 50-58. The original difference between Pennsylvania and Maryland related to *Quia emptores*, which was absolutely lifted in Maryland but only to one degree in Pennsylvania: William Penn could grant manors, but his grantees could not (Harris, p. 123). The result of this subinfeudation was that perpetual ground rents could be imposed, and were; the last known ground rent (quitrent) disappeared in 1948 (ibid., pp. 395-96).

[25]William MacDonald, ed., *Select Charters and Other Documents Illustrative of American History, 1606-1775* (New York, 1899), p. 242.

might begin to pay. Specific restrictions were also placed upon the Georgia landholders. Negro slavery was forbidden, since it was hoped that the insolvent settlers would redeem themselves through honest labor. As every settler was also to be a soldier, land inherited was entailed to male descendants only. Since strict rules were made to inhibit the growth of large estates in Georgia, the exclusion of females from inheritance was thought to be a wise measure to avoid estate consolidation through marriage.[26] Moreover, since the Georgia colonists had already demonstrated a degree of financial incompetence in England, unlimited alienation of land was forbidden; the colonists should not be tempted to engage in financial speculation. All these restrictions failed and were removed shortly, but they showed a willingness on the part of the crown to change the terms of settlement in a case like Georgia, which was planned as a charitable enterprise.[27]

Such, briefly, were the origins, rationale, and planting in America of the tenure of free and common socage. This was the carrot, the spur, the enticement for the sturdy frontiersman to go out and get his own land. He could keep it. There was a permanent tenure providing he met the incidents of it, fixed and certain. From examination of these few terms of the charters alone, we can easily see that the English colonization of America was in specific forms, even narrower than the set of possibilities that existed in England. The evolution of these controls over land use as the colonies moved toward 1776 and the rupture of the English integument was partly determined by the internal possibilities of the tenure itself, but partly also by colonial resistance to the burdens of even free and common socage—the quitrents, reliefs, etc. The colonists, knowing a minimum of English law, took a large view of it, adapted it to their own requirements—"as near as may be to the laws of England"—and in so doing began making those departures in politics and economics which gave the colonies a distinctive

[26]Charles C. Jones, *The History of Georgia* (Boston, 1883), 1:88-112.

[27]The Georgia charter began: "Whereas we are credibly informed, that many of our poor subjects are, through misfortunes and want of employment, reduced to great necessity, insomuch as by their labor they are not able to provide a maintenance for themselves and their families . . ." (MacDonald, p. 256).

American flavor, different from England.[28] In the end, they came to believe that the fixed and certain exactions on their tenures, even quitrents, were somehow illegal and, when the Revolution came, refused to pay them and abolished them—except for a few artifacts in Maryland and Pennsylvania and the peculiar case of New York.

We have seen by what right the land was taken and granted. Now let us examine the condition, on the ground, whereby these general powers and rules led to the establishment of farms and settlements. For it is in the small detail that the mechanism of social control of colonization produced the agricultural basis of the colonial economy.

[28]Paul Samuel Reinsch, "English Common Law in the Early American Colonies," *Select Essays in Anglo-American Legal History* (Boston, 1907), pp. 369-71. I do not mean to imply that more change would not be necessary to adjust the colonial property right in real estate to the realities of a changing economy as the dynamic American economy developed after independence. See Morton J. Horwitz, "The Transformation in the Conception of Property in American Law, 1780-1860," *University of Chicago Law Review* 43 (1973): 248.

Part III

England in the New World

6

Planting the Tenures and Inheritance

What we now want to examine is a very simple thing: we want to observe the historical circumstances in which the system of property right in land was established; to use the very apt word of the time, we want to see how this planting took place. Like archeologists examining potsherds, we are interested in the relationships of small objects to the larger historical issues. The beginnings of colonial America were small indeed. We will see how number and entry were controlled by the way the tenures were planted. We will see also that the ultimate prices of land and the nature of land use became far more difficult to control in the long run as the colonists realized that the land beyond the mountains might also be open to them if less restrictive policies prevailed.

One cannot read of the first landfalls at Jamestown or Plymouth without some tearing at the heartstrings. How hard it was! The colonists had no extensive experience with the range of problems they faced. The first successful grain crop was corn, and it had to be learned from the Indians—after the failure of English wheat. The first work was usually desperate communal effort, the need to build some sort of shelters for people and animals and defenses against enemies real and potential. The very life of the early colonies could be measured in terms of dwindling imported foodstocks as anxious eyes watched the potential corn harvest. In Plymouth the religious discipline carried the colonists through. In Virginia it took the imposition of harsh martial law based upon torture and profligate infliction of the death penalty to preserve the colony. The uncertain supply ship lifeline from home was an uncomfortable reminder of the frailty of the settlements. Indian massacres and disease added to the misery and hardship. It is remarkable that the English framework underwent so little permanent change in the early years. In our own time circumstances less harsh are commonly used to justify the establishment of open-ended military dictatorships, of all varieties. The power of the early seventeenth-century English law is an astonishing thing to observe, even at the distance of nearly four centuries.

Virginia, under the charter of 1606, was only partly a private venture. There was a general council in London, whose members were appointed by James I, and he also appointed from among the colonists the resident councils. Since there were two Virginia companies, one in London and the second in Plymouth, the system probably could not have worked long.[1] The Jamestown settlement of 1607 was made under auspices of the London Company. Its organization was not unlike a system of royal farms. The laborers were servants of the company, worked in gangs on the common enterprises of clearing, planting, and building. Their product went into a common store, and in return they were supposed to receive their subsistence plus some small share of the profits. The tragedies of the first settlers are well known. Of the 143 colonists who set out from London in December 1606, 50 were dead by the fall of 1607. The renowned Captain John Smith finally set the colonists to planting corn under his dictum "he that will not work shall not eat," and when he left the colony in the fall of 1609, the imported livestock had begun to flourish and forty acres of corn were growing. There followed the arrival of a new supply of ill-provided colonists and the "starving time." Of the 490 colonists alive in the fall of 1609, only 60 remained alive in June 1610 when Lord Delaware, the governor under the new charter of 1609, arrived with fresh supplies and people and saved the remnant from abandoning the enterprise.[2] The original livestock had all disappeared. With the new men and livestock a fresh start was made. The new charter made the London Company self-perpetuating, largely self-governing, like the Muscovy Company of Elizabethan times, "one Body or Commonality perpetual," and the power to organize and govern was concentrated.

Lord Delaware imposed specific work rules and seems to have made the first experiment with individual ownership of private "gardens" beyond the communal agricultural undertakings; when the new governor, Sir Thomas Dale, arrived in May 1611 with more supplies and colonists, he mentioned finding "no corn sett,

[1] Thorpe, *Federal and State Constitutions*, pp. 3383-86.

[2] Herbert L. Osgood, *The American Colonies in the Seventeenth Century* (New York, 1904), pp. 29-68; Alexander Brown, ed., *The Genesis of the United States* (London, 1890), pp. 328-32, 402-13, 413-15.

some few seeds put into a private garden or two." Dale reorganized the colony's affairs, and perhaps learning something of the colony's experience, he assigned "private gardens for each man." In these small gardens, described in his letter to the Council of 25 April 1614, is the first solid evidence of individual ownership in English America.[3] Dale was an energetic governor, ruling with martial law, and under his iron hand the colony grew until he left it in 1617.

Under the 1609 charter there was supposed to be no private land or trading for seven years, but after that there was to be the first division of the land, *pro rata.* Upon this first division, the shareholders in London were to receive 100 acres for each purchase of a bill of adventure for £12.10.0, and they were also to share in the profits. On the second division of the land, each was to receive an additional 100 acres per share. The majority of the settlers were indentured servants of the company, bound for varying terms (probably three to seven years, although no written evidence appears to remain of the earliest indentures). When his term expired, each was to be given an individual holding of 100 acres on the first division and a like amount on the second. Entry thus could be by labor as well as purchase in early Virginia. Direct grants were made for emigration and support of emigration; every person going to Virginia independently received a claim on a headright grant of 50 acres, and a similar grant for every other person he transported who remained three years (or died en route). Such transported persons had to be furnished with a year's supply of food, tools, and arms. Thus a man in London who had financed ten colonists for a year owned 500 acres of Virginia when the land was distributed; until then he had a claim on the company. From the beginning it was assumed that the corporate control and communal farming were merely temporary expedients to start the colony.[4]

Even though the first general division of the land was in fact made not in 1616 but in 1618, it was announced in London in April 1616 that the company was ready for its first land dividend.

---

[3] Brown, pp. 491-93; see also, Bruce, *Economic History,* 1:206; Edmund S. Morgan, "The First American Boom: Virginia 1618 to 1630," *William and Mary Quarterly,* 3d ser., 28 (1971): 169.

[4] Bruce, 1:502-12.

According to the announcement, the colony now prospered: "They sow and reape their corne in sufficient proportion . . . their Kine multiplying already to some hundreds . . . every man hath house and ground to his owne use, and now being able to maintaine themselves with food." But the initial distribution was announced for only fifty acres per share "till further opportunitie will afford to divide the rest, which we doubt not will bring at least two hundred Acres to every single share." In accordance with their power to grant a tenure less than or equal to their own: "every man's portion allotted to him shall be confirmed as state of inheritance to him and his heyers for ever . . . in Socage Tenure and not in Capite."[5]

As we have seen, this title was perfected not only for inheritance but for devise (by a will) as well. Thus Virginia grantees received the freest tenure they were likely to get from the English crown in that period. In 1625 the crown took over the colony and imposed a perpetual quitrent on all the land that had been granted, an exaction that was never paid in full but whose burden was consistent with socage tenure and served to remind the colonists whence came their individual right to own land.[6]

Even though general private land ownership was not granted until 1618, in 1616 the servants of a settlement called Charles Hundred were given their freedom and seem to have received it along with their land dividends that year. They were apparently the second case of individual ownership in Virginia. It is probable that their lands were encumbered with fixed obligations like those of the tenants holding leased company lands before 1618, who were obliged to contribute labor of one month each year to the company (except at seedtime and harvest).[7] Those servants who

<hr />

[5] Brown, pp. 775-79.

[6] Philip A. Bruce, *Institutional History of Virginia in the Seventeenth Century* (New York, 1910), 2:575-80.

[7] Bruce, *Economic History*, 1:210, 220-27. The date of the first actual distribution seems uncertain. One much-cited source dates it categorically as 1615—George Chalmers, *Political Annals of the Present United States from Their Settlement to the Peace of 1763* (London, 1780), p. 36: "Fifty acres of land were granted, in 1615, to every adventurer and his heirs. . . . Thus the tenure at will was changed to that of common soccage." See also Harris, *Origin of Land Tenure System in U.S.*, pp. 181-82. Morgan, p. 169, accepts 1618 as the date. I am following his article since it is the most recent and authoritative scholarship.

were entirely in the company's employ worked on the common lands and projects and were allowed to keep one-twelfth of their earnings above subsistence. After 1618 and until the crown took over in 1625, indentured servants who were farmers and worked the company's land (not in the common fields, or "garden") were furnished with a year's provisions, tools, and indentured for seven years on condition that they turn half of their product over to the company. At the end of their indentures they received a grant of land.[8] Until then they were sharecroppers.

In 1618 the company's land was generally distributed and individual private ownership was thereafter available to all who had earned land by their service, were granted it outright by the company or by the crown, bought it by purchasing shares, or were granted it by headright. On June 22, 1620, the Council for Virginia published in London *A Declaration of the State of the Colonie* in which it was boasted that in that year twelve hundred settlers already had sailed for Virginia and another thousand were waiting to go. "The colony beginneth now to have the face and fashion of an orderly state, and such as is likely to grow and prosper. The people are all divided into severall Burroughs, each man having the shares of land due to him set out, to hold and enjoy to him and his Heires."[9]

With that beginning other forces began to act upon Virginia agriculture, and the independent yeoman with his socage tenure acres quickly faded from view. The reasons were primarily tobacco and headright land grants. The culture of tobacco began in 1612, and it soon became the staple crop. To ensure the food supply, Governor Dale had placed an annual rent of 2½ barrels of grain per man upon certain 3-acre plots that had been leased to individuals in the early years; by 1616 no man was allowed to plant tobacco until he had planted 2 acres of grain. This law was still enforced in 1649.[10] The rapid absorption of land for tobacco raised fears for the food supply. Tobacco required intensive labor and fresh land at frequent intervals. The system was a feedback mechanism. The

[8]Bruce, *Economic History*, 1:310.

[9]Peter Force, *Tracts and Other Papers Relating Principally to the Origin, Settlement and Progress of the Colonies in North America* (Washington, D.C., 1844), p. 5 of item V, which also contains the names of the Virginia adventurers and a summary of the colony's principal business to date.

[10]Bruce, *Economic History*, 1:210, 214, 337.

land upon which to employ the labor was made available by the acquisition of the labor itself. Every servant imported was worth a headright land grant of 50 acres; so was every Negro slave. There was apparently no legal limit to the amount of headright land an individual could accumulate. Since the tobacco plant quickly exhausted the land, the need for fresh clearing was a steady inducement to import more indentured servants and slaves, and landholdings grew accordingly.[11] Even though the tobacco patch under cultivation at any time might be small, the need to clear new land to move the patch gave the process the characteristics of scale economies in the uses of land and labor. This need was readily apparent in the way the sizes of the estates grew. Already in 1626 most estates were from 100 to 150 acres. By 1650 the average was 446 acres, and by 1700 it was 674 acres, with seven ranging up to 10,000 acres. Such calculations do not include the Northern Neck area which had been granted to a few individuals and where, by the end of the seventeenth century, the Fitzhugh family estate was some 20,000 acres and the Howard estate was about 30,000 acres.[12]

The Virginia Company energetically sought emigrants, even shipping women over to be wives and buying London orphan boys as apprentices and shipping them too. Ninety girls, "young and uncorrupt," were shipped in 1620 at a price of 100 pounds of tobacco each. In 1621 another sixty, "handsome and recommended for virtuous demeanour," were shipped at 150 pounds of tobacco each. James I sent out a hundred convicts, a practice the Virginians did not welcome.[13] Migrants who came with families were provided houses and fenced lands. Every effort was made to attract persons with skills and trades—after the first disastrous shiploads of "jewelers, goldsmiths and profligates" had gone down to starvation and disease. Skilled tradesmen were relieved of most agricultural labor.[14] The company records for 1619 show that freedom was granted to a group of Polish servants because of their

---

[11]Ibid., 1: 512-27, 585-86, 2:78; Harris, pp. 194-236.

[12]Bruce, *Economic History,* 1:527-28, 531-32.

[13]Chalmers, p. 46; Bruce, *Economic History,* 1:593-94, 605, 612.

[14]Bruce, *Economic History* 1:215, 217.

skills at producing tar and pitch, with a proviso, informed by an eye on the local mortality rates, that in order to insure that the skills of these colonists "shall not dye with them, it is agreed that some young men shalbe put unto them to learne their skill and knowledge therein for the benefitt of the Country hereafter."[15]

Vigorous, if largely unsuccessful, efforts were made to create towns. But the power of tobacco, which even became the medium of exchange and finally was made acceptable for payment of taxes and quitrents (when paid), turned the Old Dominion into a colony of widely dispersed farms and plantations. By 1700 the greater part of the five million acres previously granted in Virginia had never been cleared or cultivated. Not only was every immigrant worth 50 acres of headright land, but he was so to each and every purchaser of his indenture, so it was not uncommon for as many as 200 acres of land to be "sued out" for a single indentured servant by the shipmaster, bondsman, merchant, and finally the farmer in Virginia.[16] By sale, adventure, royal preference, and headright grant, the land of Virginia was taken up under economic pressures which produced, in the end, large-scale holdings in a country started with small holdings. Socage tenure in Virginia became the tenure of large holdings. But in Massachusetts such was not the case. Beginning with Plymouth, Massachusetts became a colony of relatively small holdings.

In several respects the Plymouth Colony's origins resembled those of Virginia. The original agreement of 1620 was similar to the 1609 Virginia charter and was under the auspices of the current London Company (which actually did not have title to the land upon which the settlers landed). Adherence to the scheme in subsequent years molded the colony's development in interesting ways, even after major departures had been made, perforce, in adapting government and land distribution to local conditions. There was, in addition, 'a long and vexing problem involving the charter of the colony, which was settled only in 1629 when the

---

[15] Kingsbury, *Records of Virginia Comapny*, pp. 251-52.

[16] Bruce, *Economic History*, 2:495-523; Bruce, *Institutional History*, 2:576-78. The difficulty of collecting quitrents on unimproved land in the Virginia colony was finally recognized officially in 1773 when they were abolished except in the Northern Neck (Thomas Perkins Abernethy, *Western Lands and the American Revolution* [New York, 1937], p. 191; Harris, pp. 90-91).

colony was handed over to William Bradford as the major proprietor with eight associates, on the consideration of the royal fifth
of precious metals, plus another fifth promised to the Council of
New England, holders of the governing patent. In 1640 Bradford
handed his patent over to "the Freemen of this Corporation of
New Plymouth," reserving only his own farm and the lands
already settled on the "Old Planters."[17] The town of Plymouth,
like other New England townships, became itself a landholder,
distributing land according to its own lights.

Originally, a totally communal effort of seven years' duration
was planned. Then, as in the Virginia scheme, a division was to be
made. Poverty caused the Leyden separatists (the "Pilgrim
Fathers"), in exile in Holland, to conclude a contract with English
capitalists. Shares in the company sold for £10 each, every
colonist over sixteen was to receive one share, and they could also
buy shares. Those aged ten to sixteen were rated at half a share
each; those under ten received no share but were to be granted
fifty acres of uncultivated land when the distribution was made.
For seven years all net gain was to remain undistributed.[18] The
tenure was the Virginia tenure. The same tenure was specified in
the charter of the Council for New England, which in late 1620
granted the area in which the Pilgrims had settled to Sir
Ferdinando Gorges and his associates. The tenure was of "free and
common Soccage."[19]

William Bradford's journals have supplied posterity with a
superb and detailed account of the colony's early days, its terrible
suffering (half died the first winter, leaving fifty-two people only
alive), and the subsequent evolution. The colony was divided
among nineteen families, with single men allotted out among
them. Town lots were distributed, and family garden plots were
assigned. Each family was to build its own house. Communal labor
was assigned for public works, buildings, fortifications, clearing,
and planting. Agriculture was not successful until communal

---

[17]Thorpe, pp. 1841-44, 1862. Harris (pp. 104-5) dates Bradford's gift as 1641.

[18]John H. Goodwin, *The Pilgrim Republic* (Boston, 1888), pp. 52-53; J. A. Doyle,
The English in America: The Puritan Colonies (London, 1887), 1:54-56; Osgood, pp.
110-12.

[19]Thorpe, p. 1834.

efforts were abandoned and the colonists adopted the Indian method of planting corn, fertilized by fish buried in each hill (a weir was built to trap shad for this purpose). By the summer of 1622 the survivors at Plymouth were subsisting mainly on shell-fish. Bread procured from a passing fishing vessel was held in the common store and rationed at four ounces a day per person.[20] That year's harvest was disappointing, and the settlers were near starvation. In the spring of 1623, Bradford, now governor of the colony, determined to change the agricultural system so "they might raise as much corne as they could, and obtaine a beter crope than they had done, that they might not thus languish in miserie." The governor and his advisors, who were technically committed to seven years without a land division, finessed the problem and "gave way that they should set corne every man for his owne perticuler, and in that regard trust to them selves; in all other things goe on in the general way as before. And so assigned to every family a parcell of land, according to the proportion of their number for that end, only for present use (but made no devission for inheritance), and ranged all boys and youth under some familie.'"[21] Full socage tenure could not yet be given, and was not. The land could not be inherited. This innovation was, like the private gardens of Jamestown, the change that ended famime.

But there was still a hungry summer ahead. A new supply of colonists in the ship *Anne* was appalled literally to tears by Plymouth. They agreed to live a year on their own stores, until they could raise crops of their own.[22] But, as Bradford said, individual holdings "made all hands very industrious, so as much corne was planted then other waise would have bene by any means. . . . The women now went willingly into the feild, and tooke their litle-ones with them to set corne." He went on at length to excoriate the "vanitie" and "conceite" of Plato and more recent theorists who held that communal effort was superior to that of individuals, for the "common course" in agriculture at Plymouth had failed in the best of circumstances, "amongst godly and sober

[20]Goodwin, pp. 104-5; Osgood, pp. 111, 206.

[21]William Bradford, *History of Plymount Plantation, 1620-1647* (Boston, 1912), 1:299, 300.

[22]Ibid., pp. 314-15, 322-23.

men.''[23] According to the record, some planters even had surplus corn to sell by 1623.[24] The specter of famine ended, and private property at Plymouth achieved what Governor Dale's gallows and racks did in Virginia. When the land division in Plymouth came in 1627, these first allotments were changed to free and common socage, "the former division made unto the possessors thereof and to their heires forever."[25] Newly divided lands carried the same permanent tenure under the terms of each successive Plymouth charter.

The Plymouth Pilgrims were adept at the commercialization of communal property. Two examples will suffice, the cattle distribution and the trade syndicate. In both cases the problem was to harmonize private holdings with the continued "common course" in the colony's other affairs. There is no doubt that the success of each depended upon the other. The parallel existence of both kinds of enterprise reflects the fundamental dichotomy of colonial settlement, communal enterprise representing the necessary organization of society and nascent capitalism, the drive for greater efficiency.

In 1624 the ship *Charity* brought in a bull and three heifers. They were placed under a keeper. A year later four more heifers came, and the colony, with one calf, had nine animals. By 1627 the colony had twenty-seven cattle, a number of goats, and an abundance of pigs. The "common course" still ruled in sharing the benefits of these animals. The population was divided into twelve groups. The pigs were apparently divided up and granted to the groups outright. The cows were assigned. For example, to Captain Miles Standish and his company "fell the red cow which belongeth to the poor of the Colony; to which they must keep her calf of this year, being a bull, for the company." Another group got the cow "Raghorn," and another the "Blind Heifer." Commerce was at work, though, and the shares could be traded and sold. The

[23]Ibid., pp 300, 301-2.

[24]Goodwin, p. 247; but compare his evidence with Winslow, in Bradford, pp. 301-2, n.3, p. 373 n.1.

[25]*Records of the Colony of New Plymouth in New England*, ed. Nathaniel B. Shurtleff et al. (Boston, 1855-61), 9:4. Obviously the first land division has been misunderstood by earlier writers; cf. Doyle, who thought the division included the tenure (p. 78).

records show that on January 30, 1628, Edward Winslow sold his family's share of 6/13 of a red cow to Standish for £5.10.0 in corn. Abraham Pierce sold his share, together with that of Thomas Clarke, to Standish for two ewe lambs (there is no record of how the sheep got to the colony). In these deals it is believed that Standish was trading for claims to a whole cow in preparation for his project to leave Plymouth and begin a new settlement at Duxbury.[26]

Private trading based upon the distributed land also engaged the colony's basic financial existence and its commerce. The debt to the London adventurers was not paid, and the colony's title was not clear. Until Bradford got a charter in his own name, Plymouth was a legal anomaly. In 1627 the remaining forty-two London adventurers, seeking a way out of these dilemmas, offered to sell their shares for £1,800, to be paid at £200 per year. Eight of the leading colonists, led by Bradford, formed a syndicate and bonded themselves to pay the debt (risking debtor's prison if they failed). These eight, the "undertakers," then formed the colony itself into a joint-stock venture of equal partnership. The shareholders, some 256 persons (a single share for each head), were obligated to pay their *pro rata* shares of the debt payments that the colony's trade would not cover. These purchasers now owned the common property of the colony, and they made a deal with the syndicate. Their shares of the debt payment were to be met by the output of their private lands. The syndicate agreed to supply the colony with £50 of London goods each year, to be sold at agreed prices, for the credit of corn delivered at similar prices, on condition that the entire foreign trade be left in the syndicate's hands. The communal property, in trade goods, trading posts, stores, and a pinnace, a shallop, and a barque, were turned over to the syndicate.[27] A visiting emissary from New Netherland, Isaak de Rassières, made a report describing the scheme. Each family's surplus corn was sold to the governor at the agreed price for corn credit. This corn was shipped to the Indian trading posts and traded for furs. These skins, in turn, and other trade goods were shipped to London. Any deficit against the debt payment was levied directly on the colonists according to their share basis, minus the value of their corn

[26]Goodwin, pp. 292-301.   [27]Ibid., pp. 289-303.

credits. Proceeds were used to pay on the debt. The London goods were to be provided by the syndicate each year no matter what; it was their risk. It appears that land in the colony was given at this point on a per capita or, rather, a per share basis (no shares or land were given to the colony's twenty-odd indentured servants): "They apportion their land according as each has means to contribute to the . . . [debt] . . . which they have promised to those who sent them out, whereby they had their freedom without rendering an account to anyone; only if the King should choose to send a governor general, they would be obliged to acknowledge him."[28]

Even though the syndicate eventually engaged more London partners, one of the Plymouth colonists usually went to London with the furs. After a ragged history of both misfortune and deceit among the London partners (and at least one sainted Pilgrim), the debt was cleared in 1646, a quarter of a century after it was contracted. Since the debt had been indirectly a charge on all private land in the colony, the price of land in the Plymouth Colony by cash purchase would have been low, had there been any buyers.

In 1640, as noted nearlier, Bradford gave power to grant permanent land tenure to the Plymouth Corporation, as the freemen styled themselves. He kept only his farmlands, as did his associates. By then new townships had been formed with their lands, churches, and governments under the authority of Plymouth. There were no great estates as in Virginia, although of course, Bradford could have reserved such to himself, along with ground rents and other perquisites. But Bradford did not exact even the limited payments due him. Moreover, he specified that "new planters" were to receive lands from Plymouth with the same tenure the Old Planters had. The continuation of individual farms was thus provided for.[29]

By then the Massachusetts Bay Colony to the north of Plymouth had expanded out from Boston harbor on the basis of township government too, granting lands to individual families in church congregations with a stern eye upon any tendency for individuals to rise too high. There were no great estates at the

[28]Ibid., p. 309.   [29]Thorpe, p. 1862.

beginning of the City on a Hill. Bradford's bequest of his charter was thus in keeping with the nature of his social environment, as well as with the egalitarian traditions of Plymouth. Cotton Mather was impressed: "Among many Instances thereof, let this one piece of *Self-denial be told for a Memorial to him, wheresoever this History Shall be considered.* The Patent of the Colony was taken in *his* name . . . To William Bradford, *his Heires, Associates and Assigns:* But when the number of *Freemen* was much Increased, and many *New Townships* Erected, the *General Court* there desired of Mr *Bradford,* that he would make a Surrender of the same into *their Hands,* which *he* willingly and presently assented unto . . . reserving no more for himself than was his *Proportion,* with others, by *Agreement.*"[30] Mather noted that Bradford had forsaken all when he left England to answer the Lord's calling and had been rewarded with a new earthly estate, children, and a second wife. It is convenient for American history that Bradford was not tempted to use his proprietorship in a feudal manner. It would have been unseemly in the presence of Plymouth's powerful neighbor and its social and economic institutions, which did not run to feudal magnates.

The histories of Massachusetts Bay and Plymouth colonies eventually merge with a single charter in 1691. The Bay Colony has always fascinated historians for the vigor and apparent originality of its ways. There is no doubt that when John Winthrop and his Puritan colleagues left England, taking their charter with them, they intended to treat heuristically the constraint that their laws "be not contrarie or repugnant to the Lawes and Statuts of this our Realme of England." They left England precisely to stop living by such laws. In 1639 the Massachusetts colony was engaged in a grass-roots attempt to codify its laws, an effort which was crowned with success in 1641. Winthrop was opposed to excessive publicity on certain matters of domestic importance; he preferred the gradual acceptance of practice as common law to the sudden finality of the statute book. "For that it would professedly transgress the limits of our charter, which provide we shall make no laws repugnant to the laws of England, and that we are assured we must do. But to raise up laws by practice and custom make no

[30]*Magnalia Christi Americana,* bk. 2, p. 5.

transgression; as in our church discipline, and in matters of marriage, to make a law that marriages shall not be solemnized by ministers, is repugnant to the laws of England; but to bring it to a custom by practice for the magistrates to perform it, is no law made repugnant."[31]

Land distribution in Massachusetts was certainly unlike that in England, and when Andros took over New England in 1686 for James II, he held that one practice of New England was repugnant. No corporation was empowered to create a corporation in English law; therefore, said Andros, a land title granted by a New England township under authority of the "one Body Corporate and Politique in Fact and Name . . . The Governor and Company of the Massachusetts Bay in Newe-England" was no title at all.[32] In this case, unlike Winthrop's petit lesson on law evasion, the practice was based upon a statute. The Massachusetts patent was a very strong one. The governor and company were given the land by royal charter in "free and common Soccage, and not in capite, nor by Knightes Service." The only consideration given was the royal fifth. Within the range of socage tenure the company had a free hand regarding land acquisition and disposal; it was authorized "to have, take, possesse, acquire, and purchase any Landes, Tenements, or Hereditaments, or any Goodes or chattels, and the same to lease, graunte, devise, alien, bargaine, sell and dispose of, as other our liege People of this our Realme of England, or any other coporacon or Body politique of the same may lawfully doe."[33] This grant was interpreted liberally.

The Bay Colony began moving people and supplies to Salem in 1628, and in June 1630 Winthrop arrived in a fleet of eleven ships. At least a thousand people came over the ocean that year. The Salem colony had suffered terribly with the initial mortality rates that characterized these early ventures, and the new multitude of settlers moved from overcrowded Salem to the Charles River and then to Boston the next year. The poorness of the land brought a rapid dispersal of population. By June 1631 there were at least eight Puritan settlements around the bay, organized by towns, or

---

[31]*Colonial Laws of Massachusetts,* pp. 7-8.

[32]Doyle, 2:304-8.   [33]Thorpe, pp. 1848, 1852.

townships, as at Plymouth.[34] Granting land for such numbers and in such haste obviously was best done by the local authority. A Massachusetts act of 1630 anticipated the need and set forth the core of this colony's practice: "the free men of every town, with such others as are allowed . . . shall have the power to dispose of their own lands and woods . . . to grant Lots, and also to chuse their own Particular Officers, as Constables, Serveyors for the High-Wayes."[35]

Under the agreements reached before embarkation from England every shareholder was granted 200 acres for each £50 invested. If he emigrated, there was also a headright grant of 50 acres for the shareholder and one for each member of his family, a similar amount for each emigrant who was not a shareholder, and the same for each servant after his service was completed. Unlike Virginia and Plymouth, there was no specified period of common toil (impractical for such numbers) before a division of the land was made. Entry could also be made by purchase at the original fixed price. A proposal was made and rejected that the land tenures of the nonshareholders should be encumbered with hereditary services—consistent with the feudal origins of the socage tenure.[36] Whatever else can be said of the Massachusetts theocracy, it had no sympathy, in its early days, for feudal land practices, as Summer Chilton Powell has documented brilliantly in *Puritan Village*. In fact, the 1641 code known as the Body of Liberties, in article 10, disposes of the feudal element from land conveyance altogether. "All our lands and heritages shall be free from all fines and licenses upon Alienations, and from all hariotts, wardships, Liveries, Primerseisins, yeare day and wast, Escheates, and forfeitures, upon the deaths of parents or ancestors, be they naturall, casuall or Juditiall."[37]

Since there was no proprietor or royal governor, provision was made in 1646 for reversion of land to the "publick Treasury" of the colony upon failure of heirs.[38] The same is true in the United States today; escheatment in the extreme case of the existence of no heirs at all is to "the people." The code of 1641 also enabled

---

[34]Doyle, 1:137-38; Harris, pp. 274-85.

[35]*Colonial Laws of Massachusetts*, pp. 195-96.   [36]Doyle, pp. 121-22.

[37]*Colonial Laws of Massachusetts*, p. 35.   [38]Ibid., p. 150.

all persons twenty-one or older and of "right understanding and meamories" to devise their lands by "wills and testaments" and to make "other lawfull alienations of their lands and estates."[39] Hence, under the system of township government in Massachusetts, the acquisition and alienation of land title was far in advance of other colonies. It is small wonder that Andros imposed a quitrent on all the land when he became governor;[40] it must have seemed particularly naked of standard and legitimate English encumbrances. The system was in fact almost the American version of fee simple, but before its time.

The origin of New England's township governments is not agreed upon. It has been variously traced to Germany, East Anglia, the vestry of the church of England, and other sources. It is clear from the law of 1630 quoted above that the idea existed among the Puritans before the reality, and indeed Plymouth already was subdividing on a township basis, beginning with the new settlement started by Standish at Duxbury in 1628. By the seventeenth century effective local government in England was already exercised by boroughs and counties, with the old towns, grouped around their parish churches, of little importance. But the towns of East Anglia and Essex could have served as models for New England. It is usually argued that the utilization of township government at the expense of the county made New England something of a throwback. It is a logical unit though, if the center of town life is to be a single church and the community insists upon an ordered social life, as was the case in New England. Here what matters is that the land-distributing township of Massachusetts was an effective instrument for the sale and settlement of town lots and farms according to known local demand and according to the laws of the charter and the colony. The spread of land ownership was relatively easy and orderly. Each township, with its selectmen, constable, tithing-man, and host of other local officials, in the English manner including fence viewers, searchers, pressed labor for road work, stone-wall building, and so forth, created a fixed mold for growth. Each town set aside land for support of a minister and for schools. According to Frederick Jackson Turner this practice "became the foundation for the system of grants of

[39]Ibid., p. 35.   [40]Doyle, 2:306-6.

land from the public domain for the support of common schools and state universities by the federal government from its beginning." New England land was vested in the colony and township, and so far as the colonists were concerned, the matter ended there.[41] Hence, to impose English land practice in 1686 Andros had to challenge every land title granted by the townships.[42]

Even though there was no system of commonality as in Plymouth or Virginia, there were common lands for pasture and wood and elaborate rules for their uses—fowling, fishing, and water rights. In some early cases land were even divided into strips and lots were drawn for the use of them. There were even suggestions of communal control over planting of crops—a curious reversion to the three-field system of medieval England, a sensible enough solution to initial colonial problems with land clearing, which could not be done readily on an individual basis. There is no solid evidence that lands were extensively rotated as in medieval England, although there is at least one suggestion that pastureland at Plymouth was rotated, and James Kent wrote that he had been told that common land was still rotated in the early nineteenth century.[43]

In many ways the most curious history of property right in land in the United States belongs to New York, and in that case, the long arm of the feudal encumbrances reached right through the epoch of the American Revolution into the 1840s. In 1846, after a long period of violence and bloodshed, legal maneuvering and constitutional changes, a new revision of the state constitution

[41]Ibid., pp. 10-22; see also, Osgood, 1:150-52, 2:424-56. Turner, *The Frontier in American History* (New York, 1921), p. 61; see also pp. 42-65 on the New England method of settlement by towns, and Thomas Jefferson Wertenbaker, *The Puritan Oligarchy* (New York, 1947), p. 44. According to Harris the grant of free land to support education was begun by the Virginia Company (p. 193).

[42]Doyle, 2:306-7.

[43]John Gorham Palfrey, *History of New England* (Boston, 1882), 1:343: "They assigned lands for cultivation and for permanant possession, and apportioned from year to year the common meadow grounds for mowing." See also Kent, 4:468. The system of assigning common lands in several New England townships is discussed in some detail in William B. Weeden, *Economic and Social History of New England, 1620-1789* (Boston, 1890), 1:60-68, and in Powell, *Puritan Village*, about Sudbury, which was an attempt to establish the open-field system in Massachusetts.

stated explicitly that the people of New York were the "original and ultimate" possessors of the land, that on failure of heirs it would "revert, or escheat to the people." Moreover, all the land was declared to be allodial; subject to escheatment, owners of land had the "absolute property" in their holdings. Thus did the sovereign people of New York finally put themselves into the seat of the king of England, and only in 1846, nearly three-quarters of a century after the Revolution. But there were other, and even stranger, words in the new constitution: "All fines, quarter sales, or other like restraints upon alienation reserved in any grant of land hereafter to be made shall be void"; no leases for periods of more than twelve years in which "shall be reserved any rent or service of any kind, shall be valid"; and, what appeared to be a masterpiece of confusion, "all feudal tenures of every description, with all their incidents, are declared to be abolished, saving however, all rents and services certain which at any time heretofore have been lawfully created or reserved."[44] The phrase "all rents and services certain" refers, of course, to the incidents of the socage tenure. Tenures of less than socage, for example, leases, could carry uncertain feudal encumbrances. These terms were oddly out of harmony with the world of James K. Polk, the Mexican War, the Mormon migration, and the annexation of the Southwest and California.

New York's long entanglement with the curiosities of medieval land tenures did not come immediately from the English, but from the Dutch. The Dutch West India Company's charter of 1621 set up a commercial monopoly which embraced New York. The company was charged to "advance the peopling of those fruitfull or unsettled parts, and do all that the service of those countries, and the profit and increase of trade shall require."[45] The lands involved were parts of Africa, America, the West Indies, and New Guinea. The Manhattan venture, begun with company servants who were little better than serfs, did not thrive. The company determined to increase the population, and in 1629 settlers were invited by a charter of "Freedoms and Privileges" to settle up the Hudson from Manhattan Island. Those who established whole settlements were made feudal lords, or patroons. Each patroon

<hr>

[44]Thorpe, pp. 2653-55.   [45]Ibid., p. 60.

was granted land with extensive special privileges, including ten years' freedom from taxation, for transporting fifty or more persons over fifteen years of age and for providing a minister, a teacher, and a "Comforter of the sick." The company offered to supply Negro slaves and also arranged for generous assistance to the colonization. The company was to have a monopoly of the fur trade, and after 1633 Manhattan was granted the staple right, modeled after that of the city of Dordrecht, a power to tax all merchandise passing the island by water.[46]

The patroons were given rights to trade, fish, fowl, and even to privateer up and down the seacoast. Their lands were "holden of the Company as a perpetual inheritance." They could also dispose freely of their lands at will. The patroons thus had titles as good as the English free and common socage. The settlers of the patroons' land, on the other hand, were indentured under strict terms, "bound to their patroons" to work the lands according to agreement, and "any colonist who shall leave the service of his Patroon, and enter into the service of another, or shall, contrary to his contract, leave his service, we promise to do everything in our power to apprehend and deliver the same into the hands of [his] Patroon." An English socager was not thus bound. So the Dutch settler who was not a patroon held an inferior title to the land he worked. Under these conditions the land contract would be expected to bear in favor of the patroon, *ceteris paribus.* Moreover, the patroons were empowered to establish their own manor courts, and should any patroonship develop a city, the patroon had the power to appoint his own constables and magistrates.[47] Under these terms the agricultural development of New York began.

The result of private baronies established under a commercial monopoly by Europeans in the early seventeenth century was, not surprisingly, a social system with distinct feudal overtones. Outright serfdom had disappeared from Holland by then, but feudal land tenures involved far more than mere villeinage, as we have seen. The system of New Netherland has been described as

[46]MacDonald, *Select Charters,* pp. 44, 50; John Romeyn Brodhead, *History of the State of New York* (New York, 1859), 1:194-98, 243.

[47]MacDonald, pp. 47-48.

"monopoly, servitude and aristocratic privilege."[48] In 1630 Killian van Rensselaer bought an estate of some 700,000 acres and established Rensselaerswyck. His sons emigrated to found the American dynasty.[49] Others followed, and by 1634 the patroons were contesting, successfully, the company's rights to authority within the patroonships.[50] In 1664, when the English took over, the patroonships were recognized to be manors. Englishmen came into possession of some Dutch land, and by land grants new English holdings of large scale were created and the Dutch practices regarding leases, land sales, rents, and other feudal usages continued. Without actual legal tests the customs fit easily enough into the duke of York's tenure of free and common socage, and the agrarian traditions of the manor counties continued decade after decade. In 1777 the Revolutionary constitution of New York adopted the common law of England and the statute law before October 14, 1775, both of which accommodated the incidents and encumbrances that had been consistent with socage tenure in New York. In addition, all the land grants of George III and his predecessors made before 1775 were accepted.[51] This constitution acted as a conduit to pass the peculiar land tenures of the manor counties into modern American history. Connecticut in 1793, and again in 1838, passed laws designed to eliminate the incidents of the feudal tenure in that state.[52] But feudalism died harder in New York. A law of 1787—post-Revolutionary—read that no one should be discharged by the courts from payment of "any rent certain, or other services incident, or belong to the tenure in common socage, due to the people of this state, or any mean lord . . . or the fealty of distress incident thereunto." In 1830 another act of the state assembly attempting to limit feudal tenures still protected the incidents of socage: "the abolition of tenures shall not take away or discharge any rents or services certain, which at any time heretofore may be, created or reserved." A New York law of 1829 had already declared all lands to be allodial but fastened onto those fee simple holdings the incidents of the socage tenure anyhow. The courts continued to uphold these laws, and when rent services,

[48]Charles Burr Todd, *The Story of the City of New York* (New York, 1888), p. 35.

[49]Ibid., p. 36.   [50]Brodhead, pp. 247-48.   [51]Thorpe, pp. 2635-36.

[52]Kent, *Commentaries*, 4:666-67; Harris, pp. 91-97, 210-13.

those perpetual rents encompassing both fealty and real services (payment in kind), were no longer allowed, the courts held that by contract or deed a perpetual fee-farm rent could be charged on land sales, with the encumbrances attached to the New York tenures and the landlord granted the right to seize chattels against payment. These perpetual rents charged against conveyances of land were held to be mere rent charge, legal, and so the magnates of the manor counties could still tax their former lands in perpetuity.[53] There is a long list of law cases involving the Rensselaers and others to illustrate the wisdom of the courts in this matter. Finally, even after the rent wars of the 1840s, mob violence, vigilantes, bloodshed, militia action, and the 1846 revisions of the constitution, the remaining "rents and services certain" had to be paid, living on as long as the holders of those tenures did, and providing a profitable business in litigation for professional rent collectors.[54] The colonial tradition was long-lived indeed in New York State. Since land sales in New York before 1846 could involve a heavy tax to the original donor, the quarter sale, the property right in the manor counties was restricted in all respects—number, entry, price and quality. Quarter sales reduced the price received by the seller, and rent services further restricted the quality of the title conveyed.

We have already discussed the essentials of Maryland's colonial constitution, the attempted replication of the Palatine County of Durham. Lord Baltimore's fief was initially settled by the usual headright system, with land grants from the proprietor in socage tenure encumbered by perpetual ground rents. After 1683 headright grants were discontinued, and land was purchased outright from Lord Baltimore and his agents. Annual quitrents were charged, and after 1658 a fine was imposed upon entry of the new tenant with each alienation.[55] This was rent service, since it involved an oath of fealty, a legitimate encumbrance upon socage

[53]Kent, 4: 666-67, 619 n.(f), 618 N.1. Fee simple did not mean that there were no incidents of tenure, but that there were only the minimal incidents of socage.

[54]Ellis H. Roberts, *New York: The Planting and Growth of the Empire State* (Boston, 1887), p. 626; see also Henry Christman, *Tin Horns and Calico* (New York, 1945).

[55]Mereness, *Maryland*, pp. 50-52, 86. The lord proprietor was still insisting upon alienation fines in 1760.

tenure. Since *Quia emptores* had been suspended for Maryland, Lord Baltimore was free to subinfeudate his vast domain, and by 1676 some sixty manors had been established by persons other than the proprietor, averaging just under 3,000 acres, each with its little manor courts—baron and view of frankpledge.[56] Escheatment for nonpayment of quitrents was to the lord proprietor. As the years passed with indifferent management the rent rolls became increasingly inaccurate, and in 1733 the lord proprietor was reduced to offering rewards of one-third of any escheated lands discovered and first chance of purchasing the remaining two-thirds granted to the discoverer. The colonists resisted the proprietors claims to the colony's surplus lands, his desmesne lands. These were Maryland's frontier and were steadily encroached upon by settlers. Quitrents yielded insufficiently and in 1766 the proprietor ordered his manor lands sold off.[57] The attempt to create a grass-roots frontier nobility had been long given up as hopeless, and it required only the Revolution to convert the loosely encumbered socage lands of Maryland to fee simple; the end of perpetual rents, fealty, and fines in alienation had come.

The proprietary government of Pennsylvania had similar difficulty with quitrents and subinfeudation, although, as in Maryland, the proprietorship continued until the Revolution came. It was a story that need not detain us, although, let it be emphasized, the political history of Pennsylvania was another matter. The government was fundamentally progressive despite its feudal framework, and in many ways was a harbinger of the American government to come. But proprietary government and the land tenure system of colonial Pennsylvania combined to produce the familiar picture of niggling and unfulfilled obligations, as in Maryland. Unlike Maryland, by design, and Virginia, by economic forces, Penn's early emphasis on family-sized farmland grants produced a colony of sturdy yeomanry. The emphasis upon religious communities, the Germans, the Welsh, the Quakers, and so forth, like the New

---

[56]Ibid., pp. 52-53; Harris, p. 406. The reference to "leetmen" in the Fundamental Constitutions of Carolina implies view-of-frankpledge courts, and hence near villeinage in the original plans for that colony.

[57]Mereness, pp. 54, 57-69, 77-78, 85, 92-93. By the 1730s the lord proprietor was reduced to "farming" the quitrents—splitting them with professional collectors—to get them collected at all.

England township, produced moderate landholdings with the socage tenure. Some of the encumbrances lived on after the Revolution, but not for so long as nor on the scale of those in New York.[58]

In both Maryland and Pennsylvania the nonmarket control of applied nonmilitary feudalism worked indifferently. It is idle to speculate on that failure. The basis of European feudalism, a society organized to maintain military force, was missing. Had military tenures been given to warlords, as in postconquest Mexico, the story might have been different. But the feudal military institutions were nearly dead in England, and could not be, or at least were not, resurrected in America. No military tenures were allowed under the colonial charters.

South Carolina's land system is worth considering mainly because of the absurd possibilities for land tenures implicit in the phantasmagorical constitution of 1669 written by the great philosopher John Locke. In 1629 a charter was granted several proprietors, but no settlement followed. The second charter came in 1663 and launched the Carolina colony. *Quia emptores* was set aside, but a representative legislature of freemen was guaranteed. In Locke's original constitution the land was to be granted in twelve counties, each with eight seignories, eight baronies, and twenty-four colonies. There was to be one landgrave, to control territories equal to four baronies, and two caciques, each worth two baronies, in each county. These nobles were to have hereditary seats in the proposed parliament. Any holdings from 3,000 to 12,000 acres could be chartered into manors by "patent from the palatine's court."[59] It was like some comic opera in coonskin, yet the possible pile-up of permutations of fines, rents, services certain—uncertain on leases—escheatments, and what have you implicit in the scheme staggers in the mind. Locke himself was set up as a landgrave in the initial table of organization. The scheme came to little, and after 1672 settlers simply were granted free

---

[58]Hughes, *The Vital Few,* pp. 50-59; Harris, pp. 123, 220-21.

[59]The charter of 1662/63 is given in MacDonald, pp. 120-25. The guarantee of an assembly is in article 5. Locke's constitution is described in W. Roy Smith, *South Carolina as a Royal Province, 1719-1776* (New York, 1903), pp. 25-26, and printed in full in MacDonald, pp. 149-68.

socage tenures on payment of a quitrent.[60] After the colony endured several turbulent decades—eventually splitting in two—the crown took over the proprietary charter in 1729, and until the Revolution, South Carolina was simply the king's own fief, with the lands held as tenements from him, but in free and common socage on rendering of fealty and perpetual rent.[61] The assembly in its financial policies and political development was certainly as original and independent as any colonial assembly, despite its theoretical vassalage. But because of the nature of the land tenure, coupled with extensive Negro slavery, the movement toward unencumbered fee simple lands was not so marked as in, say, Maryland. The receiver general noted in 1744 that he collected about one-third of the amount of quitrents due, an impressive performance.[62]

The final interesting example of the establishment of land tenure in real property is Georgia. In no other case is the power of the English tradition over the colonial mind more evident than in this colony. Its main interest lies in a unique and unsuccessful attempt to control inheritance outside the common law and to limit the size of landholdings. The legal power to do all this came from Georgia's unique beginning as a charitable enterprise, the scheme of James Oglethorpe and his associates to establish a haven for imprisoned debtors while creating a buffer against the Spaniards in Florida.[63]

The colony's charter was made in favor of the "Trustees for establishing the colony of Georgia in America" and, receiving the royal seal in June 1732, was the last British colonial enterprise in that area which raised the standard of revolution and independence in 1776. Apart from its charitable objects, the colony's charter was similar to earlier patents. The land was granted to the trustees in free and common socage "as of our honour of

---

[60]W. Roy Smith, pp. 25-28, 34.

[61]Actually, until 1744 the fief was shared with Lord John Carteret, one of the proprietors under a second charter of 1665, who refused to sell to the crown in 1729. Until 1744 the king held seven-eighths and Carteret one-eighth. They were "tenants in common" of the colony, with the settlers "holden" of them (Edward McCrady, *The History of South Carolina under the Royal Government, 1719-1776* [new York, 1899], pp. 4-5).

[62]W. Roy Smith, p. 69.   [63]MacDonald, p. 236.

Hampton Court, in our County of Middlesex." The terms were reserved rents, payable to the king "yearly forever," of four shillings for every 100 acres granted, but none to be paid on any grant until ten years after settlement.[64] Even a charitable colony would have to yield something in consideration for its land. Compared to that of the other colonies, land in Georgia was hobbled. The quality of the tenure was reduced by entailment, land prices were constrained by a high quitrent, and entry was restrained, initially, by the colony's charitable objects. Moreover, at the beginning slavery was prohibited. A maximum limit of 500 acres per person was imposed to ensure that the land would not be given over to development of estates as had happened in the other southern colonies.[65] After twenty-one years the colony's government was to be organized by the crown, with all its officers appointed by that authority.[66] Each colonist was indentured to the trust for not less than four years, was also to be a soldier, and was therefore provided with arms as well as tools. At the start, then, Georgia appears to have been the most thoroughly constrained colony in its property rights in real estate.

The trustees, exercising the right to grant estates with tenures less than their own, placed interesting constraints upon the tenures of all the settlers, indentured or free. Each male colonist supported by the trust was to be granted fifty acres, but not with the full rights of free socage. The land was entailed, to male heirs only; that is, it could not be sold and could not pass to females. The colonist was not allowed clear title to his land, since then there would be encouragement to mortgage or sell. Women could not be soldiers, so they should not inherit; moreover, if they did inherit, lands might be consolidated by marriage, and such land accumulation ran against the object of the scheme, to provide a life as self-sufficient planters for the surplus population of honest indigents believed to be choking the workhouses and prisons of England.

[64]Ibid., p. 242.

[65]The upper limit of 500 acres is in the charter (ibid., p. 245), an unusual provision for a charter, but the Georgia charter is itself unusual.

[66]The corporation was governed by a common council, which made the detailed rules of settlement, tenures, etc., under the powers of the charter (Jones, *History of Georgia,* 1:106, 109).

Other conditions laid on the colonists included an obligation to clear and cultivate the granted lands within fixed time limits, with the right of reentry (repossession) reserved to the trustees upon failure to meet those conditions. Also, to encourage the silk culture (a favorite ambition of colonial governments) 100 white mulberry trees were to be planted for every ten acres. Private adventurers wishing to emigrate were granted a fifty-acre head-right per servant for ten servants, and perpetual quitrent was to be paid after ten years. It was agreed that servants indentured to private adventurers should be granted twenty acres by the trustees at the end of their indentures, with whatever rents, covenants, conditions, and limitations might seem appropriate. Entailment to male heirs only was also imposed upon the private land grants, and all escheatments for failure of male heirs, or for other reasons, were to the trust. In such cases the colony's common council was abjured to have special regard, in regranting the land, for any surviving daughters; and widows were to be allowed a life tenancy of the husband's house and a dower (again a life tenancy only) of one-half of the improved lands.[67] This dower was not necessarily an improvement upon the common-law rule of one-third, because in this case, as in New England, the dower could not include wild lands—a change in the English custom to accommodate the realities of the frontier;[68] for widows might not improve wild lands, and if they did, as life tenants only, they would be in conflict with heirs or successors over valuation of such improvements.

It is interesting to see how both the logic of the socage tenure and the pressures of economic reality overrode these constraints upon property rights. Before the Revolution came, indeed within little more than a decade, the system was shattered. A portent of the future appeared even before the first settlers embarked, when, under pressures from the colonists, the trustees agreed that for a generation only, the widow's dower might be the common-law third and a colonist might name a daughter as his heir upon failure of sons. But after the first generation, inheritance of males only was to adhere.[69] The failure of the Georgia scheme is an interest-

[67] Ibid., pp. 106-9.

[68] Such changes in the rules of widow's dower were common in colonial and frontier conditions (Kent, 4:27-28).

[69] Jones, 1:114.

ing example of relative institutional cohesion in straitened circumstances. An attempt had been made to place, in a colonial world governed by English institutions, a colony partly English and partly not. In the end the innovations failed and the Englishness prevailed. Nothing so eccentric as the original Georgia colony could long survive surrounded by more advantageous institutional arrangements, a lesson learned many times in the utopian frontier communities of American history, which could not maintain cultural isolation from the rest of society. Brigham Young's Utah, a century later, makes an interesting case in point.

At first landing at Savannah all work was done in common, under Oglethorpe's direction. The 50-acre lots assigned were taken up in due course, upon condition of a perpetual quitrent of two shillings per grant. New indentured servants coming over were required to work a full year in the colony "as directed" before taking up their individual allotments. By the end of 1734 the trust had already transported 341 indentured servants and granted them 8,100 acres in 50-acre lots. By then private adventurers had taken up about 5,000 acres.[70] The Georgia enterprise seemed well established under its peculiar rules. But in 1738 the leading men of Savannah petitioned to be given full land titles and the right to introduce Negro slavery. The example of neighboring South Carolina, with its rice plantations run by 5,000 whites and 40,000 slaves, must have opened new vistas to the Georgia settlers.[71] In that year daughters were admitted to inheritance, on failure of males. The grantees were also allowed in 1749 to devise, and thus partition, their lands, so the size restrictions were obviously doomed.[72] This development was inextricably linked to the introduction of slavery, since there was insufficient white labor to be hired and extensive cultivation could not be conducted by individual families. Attempts were made by individual planters to flout the law. For example, in 1746 some half-dozen Negroes were brought in as laborers, but they were forcibly removed. Other

[70]Ibid., pp. 150-51, 172.

[71]Ibid., pp. 302-3. The undertakers of the Georgia scheme well understood from the beginning that the introduction of Negro slavery would lead to large-scale landholdings and defeat the whole enterprise (ibid., p. 111).

[72]Ibid., pp. 312-13.

planters attempted to "hire" slaves from South Carolina for terms of 100 years—life.[73] In 1748 the trustees still refused to allow slavery and stated: "as the people who continue to clamour for Negroes declare that the colony can never succeed without the use of them, it is evident they don't intend by their own Industry to contribute to its success."[74] Such persons were invited to leave the colony.

But the slave interest succeeded, and in 1749 Parliament provided for a controlled introduction of slaves into Georgia with provisos that there should be one indentured white servant for every four Negroes on any plantation and that the Negroes be taught no trades (except agricultural labor). Controls were laid down for places of landing Negroes, together with health measures and provision of religious instruction. Fines were specified for violations. The conditions were accepted by a special convention held in Savannah the same year. Importation of rum had been prohibited, and that law was now repealed, along with a sumptuary law. Following the dictates of logic, in 1750 the trustees eliminated controls over tenures. It made no sense to allow the labor input in Georgia agriculture to increase, with no change in technology, and yet to hold the land input constant. The tenures were now extended to full socage tenure, "an absolute Inheritance to the Grantees, their heirs and assigns." The trustees surrendered their charter to the crown in 1753, and in 1754 Georgia became officially a royal colony, with the annual quitrents reduced from four shillings to two shillings per 100 acres. The scale of landholdings increased; there were already over 1,000 Negro slaves and about

[73]Ibid., pp. 384, 419-20. There is a perfectly lunatic story associated with the introduction of slavery in Georgia, involving a Church of England divine, George Whitefield, a fellow of Pembroke College, Oxford, and a well-known early evangelist. On his first trip to America, Whitefield opened an "orphan house" named Bethesda in Georgia, financed by slave labor on a plantation in South Carolina. He lobbied ceaselessly for the introduction of slavery into Georgia so that it could be employed directly in his Christian adventure. After the introduction of slavery into Georgia, the orphan house grounds and farm were cultivated by a gang of slaves. The orphan house burned to the ground in 1770. Whitefield had even recruited Indian "orphans" from neighboring tribes so that his slaves would have someone to support by their labor (ibid., pp. 401-2; see also McCrady, pp. 242-49). Carl Bridenbaugh, *Cities in the Wilderness* (New York, 1963), p. 425, refers to Whitefield as a humanitarian.

[74]Jones, 1:419, n.1.

2,400 whites by 1753, and there followed from the new assembly a hair-raising set of laws controlling Negroes. It was a far cry indeed from Oglethorpe's eleemosynary utopia. In 1755 the upper limit of 500 acres was removed by the new royal governor, quit-rents on the larger estates were reduced to the same perpetual two shillings per 100 acres that applied to the smaller grants, and the assembly removed all regulations controlling the minimum rate of land cultivation, so that new land could be purchased beyond immediate plantation needs.[75] The land system was now completely commercial.

Thus property right in Georgia land was at least as great, after only three decades, as in the other colonies, despite efforts to control it by the colonial government. The fundamental social control over property right that ruled was the standard English tenure of free and common socage and its ordinary incidents, and the effort by a charitable trust to reduce it had failed. Custom and economics together proved more powerful than good intentions. It is interesting that Georgia removed entailment from its land law in its Revolutionary constitution of 1777, and also adopted inheritance by equal proportions for all children in cases of intestacy, eliminating the common-law system of primogeniture, or descent to the eldest male.[76] Other forces now were pushing against the continued existence in America of English property law. It was a century and a half since Jamestown and Plymouth.

This study of colonial property right is not complete without accounting for the laws of inheritance, since in the end, the heirs of the colonists owned the land. Here the primary institutions were wills, primogeniture, entail, the law of the double portion, and, just possibly, gavelkind.

As we have seen in chapter 5, Henry VIII's Statute of Wills allowed lands held in socage tenure to be devised. In 1677 the Statute of Frauds of Charles II, which laid down conditions for valid conveyances, deeds, and leases, also set out the precise terms of wills. For example, no will "shall be good, where the estate thereby bequeathed shall exceed the value of thirty pounds, that is not proved by the oaths of three witnesses (at least) that were

[75] Ibid., pp. 422-26, 428, 451, 459-60, 479-86, 487-88.
[76] Ibid., 2:259.

present at the making thereof, nor unless it be proved that the testator at the time of pronouncing the same, did bid the persons present, or some of them, bear witness that such was his will."[77] Wills were to be in writing, and provisions were made for trustees, debts against the estate, and so forth. Specific rules for probate and alterations were given, and provisions were included recognizing the unusual circumstances in which the last wills of soldiers and sailors might be made. Both Plymouth Colony and Massachusetts had laws governing wills before the Statute of Frauds was enacted, but that statute of 1677 was probably the law of all the colonies thereafter.[78]

The English common law of descents provided for inheritance of land by primogeniture where wills did not apply, primarily in the cases of intestates and entailments. The general rule was fairly simple. Land went to the eldest son as the heir. If he died intestate without an heir, title reverted theoretically to the last man (although deceased) who had held the title, and then descended again. If B, the eldest son of A, died without a male heir, title would go to C, A's second son (theoretically having reverted to A and descended again), and to the heir of C. Any reader of English history knows that endless complications could arise from this system. It is thought that primogeniture came to England with the Normans, and that the Saxons practiced equal division to all heirs. The object of primogeniture in theory was to endow a military vassal with land. The eldest son was the first capable of military service; he was the heir. The church had introduced wills among the Saxons, but after the Conquest devise of land by will died out for long centuries; "only God can make an heir" was the rule of English inheritance of land. Primogeniture, thought originally applicable only to lands held by knight service, gradually was attached to socage and other lower tenures.[79]

Entailment of estates, the establishment of a life tenure from the donor on condition that the estate descend intact to the next heir in line, was established in 1285 by the statute *De donis conditionalibus*. Under this rule the tenant of an entailed estate

---

[77]29 Charles II, c. 3, art. 19.　　　[78]Kent, 1:537-38, 4:96, 482, 550.

[79]Maitland, *Constitutional History of England,* pp. 30, 37-39; Holdsworth, *History of English Law,* 3:29-275.

could not alien those lands. The legal methods of getting out of this, of "docking the tail," were, even by expert opinion, remarkably obscure.[80] Usually entails were not broken. If the land was entailed, the English rules of descent virtually guaranteed perpetual succession of an estate, and hence perpetuated the great estates of England's hereditary nobility. Few estates were entailed, of course, but unless estates were devised by will, primogeniture usually ruled wherever the English laws prevailed. And that, as we have seen, was wherever the English went, colonized, formed governments, and did not create some intervening statute law. English law hovered in the background like some ancient spell. Thus the importance of the 1787 Northwest Ordinance, which broke the spell for the western lands. In that ordinance partible inheritance was the rule—equal division among males and females of equal degrees of consanguinity without regard to half blood. Elsewhere, in the original colonies, the spell lingered. Richard B. Morris, commenting upon a faulty Massachusetts law of 1920 barring estates tail, commented: "This statute does not abolish entailed estates, and in the event of the failure of the tenant in tail to convey in fee simple, the land is subject to the common law rules of primogeniture as they had evolved by 1312 in interpretation of the statute *de donis*."[81] Lord Coke wrote that the aristocracy refused to change the law of entailment because estates protected by *De donis* were not liable to be forfeit for treason or felony or for debt, for the tenant for life could not prevent the passing of the land to his heir.[82] Such estates could be seized by a parliamentary bill of attainder, an infamous device which the Americans specifically forbade in the U.S. Constitution.[83]

The law of primogeniture was the colonial rule of descent of intestates outside New England, Pennsylvania, and the Dutch settlements in New York. Generally, in Rhode Island after 1728, in most of New York, and in the southern colonies primogeniture ruled. Entailed land could exist in all the colonies (limited to male

[80]Milsom, *Historical Foundations of Common Law*, pp. 142-57.

[81]"Primogeniture," pp. 26-27.

[82]Kent, 4:11; Blackstone, *Commentaries*, bk. 2, pp. 88-89; Morris, "Primogeniture," pp. 32-36.

[83]Art. 1, sec. 9.

heirs in Georgia for a time) before the Revolution, but estates-tail—conditional inheritances—are severely limited in the United States today.[84] It was the combination of primogeniture and entail which produced the great estates of England and which was so opposed by the radicals in the revolutionary epoch.

The law of the double portion first appears in American history at Plymouth Colony. It is mentioned by de Rassières in his account of Plymouth Colony in 1627.[85] In 1641 it appeared in London in John Cotton's *Laws of New England* (never actually enacted): "If a man have more sonnes than one, then a double portion to be assigned and bequeathed to the eldest sonne, according to the law of God."[86] The latter reference is to Deuteronomy 21:17, which speaks of acknowledgment of a first son who was adopted, by granting him a double portion. The Body of Liberties of Massachusetts, adopted in 1641, mentions the double portion also: "When parents dye intestate, the Elder sonne shall have a double portion of his whole estate reall and personall, unless the General Court upon just cause alleadged shall judge otherwise." The other sons would inherit equal portions, and should there be no male heirs, daughters would inherit equally as "copartners."[87] This equal division, apart from the double portion, was defended in a document of 1646, a declaration of parallels between the laws of the Massachusetts colony and those of England, after Robert Child attacked the colony for having "no settled form of government according to the laws of England."[88] The defense of the Massachusetts law of descent was that the charter had been granted at the "Manor of East-Greenwich in our County of Kent," where the custom of descent was gavelkind, a tenure by which lands descended to all sons in equal parts. This tenure is thought to be a minor social artifact of pre-Conquest times; there were other such local customs in England that had successfully defied

---

[84]Morris, "Primogeniture," pp. 24-25; Kent, 4:12-15, 386 n.(d).

[85]Goodwin, p. 309.

[86]*Hutchinson Papers*, p. 191. It is thought that Cotton wrote the London draft of these laws about 1636 (Morris, "Primogeniture," p. 41; *Colonial Laws of Massachusetts*, p. 6).

[87]*Colonial Laws of Massachusetts*, p. 51, arts. 81 and 82.

[88]Morris, "Massachusetts and the Common Law," p. 443.

the centuries of primogeniture. There is no reason to suppose that the Stuarts realized that they were imposing gavelkind descent whenever they made out a patent from their manor at East Greenwich. But such could have been the interpretation, and it surely was not repugnant to the laws of England. Another curiosity of gavelkind was that, like the estates under *De donis,* lands in Kent were not liable to be confiscated for treason or felony. Hence the rule of tumb in Kent was, "The father to the bough, the son[s] to the plough."[89] The tenure in Kent did not include the double portion to the eldest son, but there is no reason to suppose that the Puritans did not believe their system to be in accord with gavelkind. The colonists at Plymouth did; in 1636 they enacted a law declaring "that Inheritances shall descend according to the commendable Custom Tenure and hold of east greenwich,"[90] in which they included the double portion.

The law of double portion, with equal division among all the children other than the eldest son, without regard to sex, applied in New England and Pennsylvania, while the Dutch in New York followed the Justinian Code with straight equal division. It was thus that by dropping the double portion only, Robert Dane was able to follow, as he said, the laws of Massachusetts when he wrote section 2 of the 1787 Northwest Ordinance. The rules of the ordinance became fairly general in the United States in the federal period, although there was great variation in details.[91] Jefferson, in his *Notes on the State of Virginia,* written in 1781 while the Revolution was still on, said it was intended to amend Virginia's laws "so that the lands of any person dying intestate will be divisible equally among all his children, or other representatives of equal degree."[92]

[89]Blackstone, bk. 2, pp. 62-65; Holdsworth, 3:259-75; Morris, "Primogeniture," pp. 38-40.

[90]Bradford, p. 300 n.2; see also, Morris, "Primogeniture," p. 39, and his discussion generally of the view that gavelkind ruled in Massachusetts and Connecticut (pp. 37-46). The evidence is mixed. Harris (pp. 30, 37, 152-54) takes gavelkind as a legitimate origin of Massachusetts practice, but what was done in Massachusetts, equal division between all children with a double portion to the eldest son, was not gavelkind.

[91]Harris, pp. 43-49; Kent (4:384-99) discusses the variations in state codes regarding descent in the early federal as well as in the colonial era.

[92]P. 227.

Clearly the English law of descent had only a partial hold on the colonies by the time of the Revolution, but it was not overthrown out of hand. Virginia abolished primogeniture in 1776, Georgia in 1777, North Carolina in 1784, Maryland and New York in 1786, South Carolina in 1791, and Rhode Island in 1798. The double portion was abolished in Massachusetts in 1801 and in Pennsylvania in 1810.[93] How widespread the actual practices of primogeniture and entail had been, in combination, will probably never be known. Richard Morris found an extraordinary variety of applications in his investigation of the colonial world. Since *De donis* could prevail where no other law canceled it out, or did so only defectively, one could never be certain. According to Morris, in 1927 *De donis* still applied in Illinois, Colorado, and Arkansas.[94] As Chief Justice Waite said in 1877, we changed our form of government in 1776, not the substance.[95] Estates-tail, entails, were abolished in Virginia in 1776, Georgia in 1777, New York in 1782, North Carolina in 1784, Kentucky in 1796, and New Jersey in 1820.[96] But the desire of donors to grant conditional estates meant that entail would never die out in a free society, although in the United States entails are mainly limited to a single generation only.

Such was the colonial heritage of property right in the ownership of land. It should be emphasized that the colonists also brought with the common law the whole corpus of property right in incorporeal hereditaments, bailments, estates at will and by sufferance, leases, cropping on shares, easements, mortgages, trusts, uses, joint tenancies, coparcenary, fishing rights, rights of navigation and public roads and highways, English notions of property in watercourses, servitudes, division fences and party walls, running waters, distress and distraint for debt, rights of entry and of replevin, the pursuit of wild game, as well as the whole corpus of municipal law—market controls, franchises, and controls over public enterprises and common carriers—which surrounded and buttressed the basic property right in land. When the

[93]Morris, "Primogeniture," p. 25; Kent, 4:384-99.

[94]Morris, "Primogeniture," pp. 26-27; Kent, 4:13-20.

[95]*Munn* v. *Illinois,* 94 U.S. 113 (October term 1876, which lasted until May 1877).

[96]Morris, "Primogeniture," pp. 26-27; Kent, 4:13-20.

whole mass was applied, developed, and many times simply re-enacted, it became the set of domestic rules whereby the new republic ordered its daily affairs. The same was true of laws of contract and negotiable instruments. Property right in land is only the tip of the iceberg of colonial nonmarket social control that was passed to the republic after the Revolution.

When the Revolution came, the quitrents and other incidents of the socage tenure disappeared—apart from the extraordinary cases like New York, Maryland, Pennsylvania, and possibly New Jersey, where they lingered. In the end the words themselves disappeared, since socage, stripped of its incidents and dependent upon the people for its validity, became just ownership of the land itself, the American fee simple. Writing in New York in 1826 James Kent was already insisting that the distinction was becoming blurred—even though, in that state, socage incidents still existed: "The title to lands [in the United States] is essentially allodial, and every tenant has an absolute and perfect title, yet, in technical language, his estate is called an estate in fee simple, and the tenure free and common socage."[97]

Socage tenure and fee simple had come to mean virtually the same thing, "An estate of inheritance and nothing more." Fee simple, the simple feud, formerly implied a use as a beneficiary of someone else, a usufructory estate. It carried such a meaning no longer: "Whether a person holds his estate in pure *allodium*, or has an absolute inheritance in fee simple, is perfectly immaterial, for his title is the same to every essential purpose."[98] It was the colonial experience, over a century and a half, that simplified, finally by revolution, the encumbrances of socage tenure to a near equivalence with an allodial estate. It was the American fee simple, with land a commodity largely separated from the social organism except by strict monetary measures, that enabled millions of Americans to possess the continent by making a single money payment for land, to alien and purchase it in whatever amounts they

[97]Kent, 3:647-48.

[98]Ibid., p. 670; Harris (p. 15) points out the logical error in Kent's view, showing that allodial land is not possible where the law of ownership descends from that of the English; for example, the state maintains the lord's position on nonpayment of property taxes, our modern version of quitrents.

pleased whenever they wanted it, and to use and enjoy it, so long as they paid their taxes. Taxes on land were usually dedicated to specific uses, like schools, and that was not unlike some of the uses of colonial quitrents. In a strict sense then, our method of owning real estate is what the colonial world left us. The family farm and the town lot held in fee simple were the results.

7

The Colonist and the System

It is ordered that no person, Householder or other, shall spend his time, idely or unprofitably, under paine of such punishment, as the County Court shall think meet to inflict. And the Constables of every Towne are required to use speciall care to take notice of offenders of this kind, especially of common Coasters, unprofitable Foulers, and Tobacco takers.

Colonial Laws of Massachusetts, 1633

We have seen how, by right of conquest, a system of landholding was transplanted from England to the colonies. We have further noted that only certain parts of the total English system came over with the settlers. With hindsight these appear to have been fortunate selections from the whole range of possibilities. Given the nature of the colonial enterprise, an individual ownership right that could be inherited directly, devised by will, and aliened freely upon a financial payment was appropriate to conditions that called upon the exertions of individuals to expand the area of colonization beyond the initial footholds on the wilderness shore. We saw that the colonists pushed their governments to achieve the full rights of the socage tenures where they were initially withheld and that in the self-government of Massachusetts, even the perpetual ground rent itself was not generally imposed. This all seems reasonable too: in a country where land was abundant and labor scarce, the concept of perpetual fixed and certain payments to sellers of land for the right to occupy land already owned in all other respects made no sense. The persistent refusal fully to honor the obligation of perpetual rent was more than a refusal to be taxed by this device; it was a popular rejection of an anachronism by defaulting upon its conditions. The inability of governments to collect the rents or to seize the lands in question under their legal right of reentry showed the weakness of the various English governments' control over land settlement.

It is in view of this weakness that one recognizes the logic, in the last years before the Revolution, of the British government's efforts to raise excise taxes from the colonies to help defray the expenses of royal government. This policy too failed when the Revolution swept away British authority. The old system's anachronistic character is thrown into even sharper focus by the case of New York, where, as we have seen, parts of the system, conditions granting private individuals economic rights over the land of other private individuals, lingered on into the nineteenth century. Elsewhere, the only conditions retained were those granting such rights to a government, specifically, that condition which limits property right in landowning by the obligation to pay taxes upon the land. But these taxes are owed to governments which are elected by the people themselves, and not to the lord proprietor or a remote government in England. Economically the difference may seem trivial to the harried taxpayer, but politically it has been enormous.

Other aspects of colonial economic life did not undergo so much alteration. What the colonists did to create a domestic framework of organized economic life within the total social system is easily comprehended by modern Americans, if not in substance, at least in form.

1. There was considerable control over the conditions of immigration and labor. More than half the colonial immigrants came over under strict control, not under general immigration laws but under a tighter control—an open-ended labor contract, a work guarantee. Indentured servants, who probably accounted for more than half of all the white immigrants before 1776, were required to labor for the settlers who preceded them for fixed terms of years in order to earn the right, in turn, to a permanent residence. During their years of bound service the indentured colonists labored for food and subsistence just as did the Negro slaves. The latter, who made up 14 percent of the population by 1790, had been imported under controls in the southern states, subjected to laws of grossly brutal nature in their daily lives, and of course, for the most part were bound for life, as were their children.

Thus, less than half, and perhaps not more than 30 percent or so, of the immigrants to colonial America outside New England came in free to contract a wage bargain with employers, or to enter into private employment. These, together with the descendants of earlier immigrants and indentured servants who had served their time, were responsible, on the supply side, for the development of a free market for labor. In 1790 about 97 percent of the population was engaged in agriculture, so that outside of this primary occupation only a small portion of the total labor force could have pushed against both law and custom to establish an effective labor side to the wage bargain. It is not surprising, then, that employers in the towns of colonial America continually attempted to set wages by law. In addition, there was English precedent for such laws. Wages, terms of apprenticeship, obligation to perform effectively, all these conditions of labor were early restricted by the agencies of the law for individual wage earners (and, of course, it was not until the case of *Commonwealth* v. *Hunt* in 1842, more than two centuries after the initial settlements, that the right of laborers to combine in negotiating the wage bargain was countenanced in American law).

2. There was direct consumer protection. Since the colonies were English, the customary controls over the qualities and prices of goods made and sold prevailed. The right of government to enforce strict standards of this sort had been established by written law as early as Magna Carta, had been traditionally enforced by courts in England, and was imposed in early colonial legislation. The idea that the free market might be a better social control over economic activity than government was only partly acceptable to early colonial thinking, as it was in the common law. Indeed, even in the early federal period such laws continued to be enforced. Similarly, according to English practice the very right to vend commodities was initially restricted to certain places and times. The vigorous commercial life of the colonies would finally break down many of these restrictive laws, but only in time, and many have remained. The desire to use government to control business has never disappeared in the United States. In colonial America there was long precedent.

3. There was regulation of traditional public callings. Apart from ubiquitous control over business, the kinds of regulated public callings commonly controlled in our own time by municipal

ordinances, state laws, or regulatory agencies have been controlled from the beginning. Innkeepers, publicans, public servants like ferrymen, carters, and carriers, operators of docks and wharves at seaports were never allowed to function within the colonial economy except under conditions of explicit control over quality, regularity, and prices of services. These activities fell largely under ancient English laws, and control of them was a settled part of English and colonial life.

4. The monetary sector was controlled. There were usury laws and attempts to regulate the exchange rates between domestic, English, and foreign coins. Emission of paper money by colonial governments and the establishment of banks were controlled, resisted, or forbidden. These were sources of very considerable friction, not only between the colonists and the mother country but among the colonists themselves. The traditional inflationism of the backwoods debtor, resisted by the sound money forces of the centers of merchant activity, began, apparently, as soon as colonial society produced enough economic development for such specialization and division of labor to appear in the ongoing processes of economic life.

5. There were extensive rules in the primary sectors regarding mining, fishing, timber, and agriculture. These obviously were necessary to avoid conflicting claims. On the land itself, the agricultural sector, there were rules for the operation of common lands and pastures, for surveying, partitioning, and fencing of private holdings, for the establishment of pounds for wandering livestock, for fishing rights, and for the impressment of harvest labor.

6. At the level of local government the powers of taxation were created and used, labor could be impressed for necessary social projects, men were assigned to the night watch, and conditions were laid down for the arming and maintenance of military forces.

It should not, therefore, be supposed that the rough and ready frontier life of colonial America was one of utter freedom, or even disorder and lawlessness. Quite the reverse was true, and especially so in the extreme cases, the closely knit religious settlements of New England and Pennsylvania. Economic life in colonial America was subject to nonmarket social control from the hill farm to the seaport. But the farther away they were from the seats of power, the less stringent was the effective control, and as time passed the colonists themselves began to change, to exercise greater freedom of action. Life became more openly commercial as the frontier expanded and the older system, exemplified by the Puritan towns, weakened. At the seaport, of course, it was the larger world outside the colonies that intruded, and the economic interest of the colonist became entangled with the larger interests of crown and empire. Here the colonist's own ability to influence his life was more sharply constrained, and he was subject to laws and rules that were not directly affected by his own exertions. Nor, in many cases, could his colonial government effect changes in the bases of imperial control. From 1763 onwards the crown attempted to intensify that control.

There is an interesting hypothesis to consider at this point. It has not been shown that the actual economic costs of the crown's efforts to intensify its controls after 1763 were sufficient by themselves to raise the flames of revolution. New taxes and rigid enforcement of the Acts of Trade and Navigation, or efforts in that direction, appear to have cost the colonists, directly, very little, per head of population.[1] But since the domestic system of economic control we have outlined had long been loosening up under the influence of expanded opportunities for economic activity that came with growth in the final decades of the colonial

[1]The modern discussion of this issue began with Louis M. Hacker, "The First American Revolution," *Columbia University Quarterly,* 37 (1935): 259; Lawrence Harper, "Mercantilism and the American Revolution," *Canadian Historical Review* 23 (1942): 1. An attempt to nip this discussion in the bud came in a note at the end of Charles M. Andrews's great study, *The Colonial Period in American History,* 4:425-28. He failed, and the discussion continues: Robert Paul Thomas, "A Quantitative Approach to the Study of the Effects of British Imperial Policy on Colonial Welfare: Some Preliminary Findings," *Journal of Economic History* 25 (1965): 615; Douglass North, *Growth and Welfare in the American Past* (Englewood Cliffs, N.J., 1966), ch. 3; Roger Ransom, British Policy and Colonial Growth: Some Implications of the Burden from the Navigation Acts," *Journal of Economic History* 28 (1968): 427; R. P. Thomas, "British Imperial Policy and the Economic Interpretation of the American Revolution," ibid., p. 436; Peter D. McClelland, "The Cost to America of British Imperial Policy," *American Economic Review* 59 (1969): 370; Gary Walton, "The New Economic History and the Burden of the Navigation Acts," *Economic History Review* 24 (1971): 533; see also ibid., 26 (1973) 668 for further discussion.

regime, the crown's policies could have seemed far more intolerable to the colonists than the evidence of the direct burden of the imperial system indicates. Suppose, for example, that after 1763 a massive effort had been made to bring back the full rigor of the conditions of the original land grants. Not only would the landowners of the New England townships find themselves applying for new titles, but throughout the colonies full payment of quitrents, fines, and reliefs, together with ceremonial swearings of fealty and escheatments of the land itself to the crown or the various patent holders on failure to conform, no doubt would have produced chaotic conditions. The steady rise in the ratios of usable productive resources to available manpower had loosened the constraining bonds of a system of domestic control of economic life imported from the villages and market towns of seventeenth-century England.

Such a reimposition of rigorous imperial control, irritating and perhaps costly, would also have seemed a gross anachronism. For decades after independence the system of colonial domestic control of economic life wilted away as the American economy moved westward into the new lands and the old seaports grew and prospered with a greater volume of trade and the beginnings of American manufacturing. At the same time, the governments' minimal controls were more than offset by positive efforts to enhance private opportunities through direct participation in economic expansion by financing and encouraging internal improvements, roads, canals, and harbors, at the same time that money creation was undertaken by a growing system of issuing banks. These movements were harmonious. Before the Revolution the attempt to embrace the increasing commercialization of domestic economic life by controlling the seaport economy's international life more rigorously and, after 1763, by blocking internal geographic expansion as well was inharmonious, a contradiction, as the determinists would say.

If we consider the evidence that most of the colonial restrictions over the details of economic life continued for some decades after the Revolution, but at the hands of the elected governments of the new republic, then the traditional complaint takes on greater weight, viz., that the real trouble with the government of colonial America was that it had finally become simply foreign to Americans. It was not the rigor of the control, but that the control was enforced by the British, and too many Americans no longer felt an allegiance to the crown for the imperial tie to bear the weight of dissension. When, after the Revolution, Shay's Rebellion broke out in western Massachusetts, the imposition of military force produced no new Lexington and Concord. The military force was no longer a case of foreign subjugation.

8

The Labor Contract:
Bondsmen and Slaves

In the conditions of the colonial labor contract all four of the primary areas of nonmarket control were in full force. Both the quantity of employment and entry into the labor market were rigorously restricted by colonial law and practice. The Elizabethan law, the background law of the colonies, still restricted the trades and apprenticeships, while the prevalence of indentured servitude for whites and lifelong and hereditary enslavement for blacks strictly imposed legal control on both entry and exit from those parts of the colonial labor force. Wage controls numbered among the devices for fixing the price of labor, while quality was controlled by laws enforcing satisfactory performance for both blacks and whites and, to some extent, for their owners and employers as well. The colonial labor market appears now as an ugly thing, in which market forces were primarily limited to the buyers' side of the wage bargain (and were not always present even there). Here the long arm of the colonial tradition stretched all the way to the Wagner Act in 1935 and the *Jones and Laughlin* case in 1937. Only then could it be said that the law had achieved proximate neutrality in its treatment of the wage bargain. If it can be argued that the New Deal legislators and the Supreme Court tilted too far toward the supply (labor) side of the market, there was some historical justice; it made up for the centuries when American labor was in the status of servant.

The early laws of colonial Massachusetts provide a comprehensive view of the uses of early colonial government to control the main parts of economic activity. These laws reveal an economy of primary producers—farmers, hunters, fishermen, woodsmen—who depended upon the outside world for a market and for crucial supplies. To gain these supplies the colonists utilized intermediary skills and labor—tanners, coopers, carpenters, millers, ferrymen, sailors, cartmen. It is clear that in the early days the colonists feared the consequences of free-agent contracting to sustain their economy. Moreover, the Massachusetts laws of 1641 were passed less than a century after Elizabeth's Statute of Artificers and Apprentices, which was still the basic law of England, and therefore the background law of the colonies, regarding work and wages.[1] This statute of 1562, an "act containing divers orders for artificers, labourers, servants of husbandry and apprentices," placed comprehensive controls over labor and wages. It was a blueprint for a quasi-totalitarian labor state, and has been so celebrated by historians. It is easier to understand the harshness of the rules of work in the colonies against this background.

The Statute of Artificers and Apprentices was a piece of class warfare imposed from above. Persons of wealth, born gentlemen, persons with sufficient independent incomes (the act specified the amounts), scholars, and so on, were exempted from agricultural labor, as were mariners, fishermen, miners, and those engaged in trades as masters, journeymen, or apprentices in cities, corporate towns, or market towns. Except for these people and persons eligible for apprenticeships, separated by class origins for the recognized hierarchy of organized trades, all men between the ages of twelve and sixty were to be compelled to labor in agriculture. Single women between the ages of twelve and forty were to accept services as directed by local authorities. Conditions of employment, hours of daily labor, years of apprenticeship (seven at the minimum), conditions of mobility between jobs, notices for termination of employments, minimum lengths of employments, punishments for violations—all were specified. Persons were tied to their jobs and locations down to the levels of the minor local jurisdictions of "lath, rape, wapentake or hundred" and could not leave without legal papers (the act included the exact form). Moreover, wages were to be determined by appropriate local officials—bailiffs, sheriffs, justices of the peace—and penalties were provided for violations, for either offering or accepting wages in excess of those determined. Fines and forfeitures were split between the crown and the parties successfully bringing prosecution. In other words, the poor were pressed into labor and were paid to spy upon each other.

[1] 5 Elizabeth, c. 4.

This law formed the background of initial labor relations in the colonies, and many of its features appeared in colonial laws, for example, the Massachusetts laws forbidding the harboring of strangers, requiring artisans to work in the harvest, and prohibiting employment in trades without apprenticeship.[2] Every householder was allowed one apprentice, bound for seven years, if he or she were less than twenty-one years of age. No one could "use or exercise any art, mystery or manual occupation" except after serving a seven-year apprenticeship. In England guilds handled all the administrative details of this system. It is small wonder that a people accustomed to this ironclad set of universal controls over labor should have transplanted much of it to America. What is interesting is not so much its appearance in the colonies—it was after all, the law—but the changes that came in a new economic environment and the slow evolution of a free labor contract. It is useful to remember, when considering both indenture and slavery, that even the unfettered sector of the colonial labor force was, by law and custom, liable to rigorous compulsion.

So the weight of seventeenth-century tradition was hardly the free wage bargain. But probably as important in colonial thinking was the constantly noted shortage of skilled workmen and the steady pressure on wages. Relatively, farmers were many and craftsmen few. More generally, these laws mirror a static conception of economic life. Just as the land settlement techniques of the Puritans envisaged few changes in social life—replication, over and over, of the seated township with its church and school—so the laws controlling the conditions of labor implied that labor would be so ruled. In fact these laws failed their purposes consistently, but just as consistently colonial towns continued to pass such legislation for decades.[3] There was some expectation of sub-

[2]Weeden, *Economic and Social History of New England*, 1:272-73; Wertenbaker, *Puritan Oligarchy*, p. 68; *Colonial Laws of Massachusetts*, p. 203; cf. 5 Elizabeth, c. 4, arts. 10, 11, 23, 47. David J. Saposs, writing in John R. Commons et al., *History of Labor in the United States* (New York, 1918), 1:43, thought that impressment of town labor in the harvest in colonial Massachusetts in 1646 was an American example of class discrimination; it was not more than provided for in the background law of England.

[3]Weeden, 1:334; Bruce, *Economic History* 2:415-21; Morgan, "The First American Boom," p. 175; Bridenbaugh, *Cities in the Wilderness*, pp. 49-52. An early example of an attempt by artificers to set prices and wages was among the coopers of New York in

mission, and given the law and the enforcement techniques of the era, that expectation doubtless was not entirely misplaced. Since the laws were so carefully framed in terms of property right in real estate, incorporeal property, and even in financial paper, it is clear that the worker's property right in his labor was not yet recognized, one of the classic problems in the development of modern capitalism. The Elizabethan law treats laborers much as common soldiers were treated in military life, something to be controlled and compelled to serve in the interests of the state.

Further, it is not surprising that labor should be so regulated when so many other economic activities were under strict surveillance by the Puritan theocracy. Oaths printed in the colonial laws for the offices of leather sealer, clerk of the market, apprizer, viewer of pipestaves, and viewer of fish[4] indicate but a portion of the little army of inspectors who split their confiscated goods and fines not only with the government but commonly with informers as well. Bakers of bread were liable to have their homes inspected for false-weighted loaves, and millers were limited in their charges, as were innkeepers.[5] Puritan society intervened literally in every part of life, so attempts to control wages should not surprise us. Nor, given the background, should the fact that control over wages was placed in the hands of orthodox church members and men of property: "the freemen of every Town may . . . agree amongst themselves about the prizes and rates of all workmens labour and servants wages . . . whosoever shall exceed those rates . . . shall be punished by the discretion of the court." Moreover, the community attempted to curtail labor mobility by imposing wage uniformity: "if any Town shall have Cause of Complaint against the freemen of any other Town, for allowing greater Rates or wages than themselves, the County Court of that shire, shall from time to time set Order therein." Wages could be paid in kind (usually corn is specified), with rules for determining fair rates.[6] Not only

---

1679; this attempt at unilateral wage control was struck down by the law and the offending tradesmen were fined (Brodhead, *History of State of New York,* 1:330).

[4]*Colonial Laws of Massachusetts,* pp. 203-8. Such oaths were prescribed for similar offices in England (Powell, *Puritan Village,* pp. 44-45).

[5]*Colonial Laws of Massachusetts,* pp. 124-25, 163-66, 175.

[6]Ibid., p. 174.

were wages controlled, but the artisans themselves were liable, at first, to be pressed into harvest labor (at going wages for farm laborers).[7] Impressment for road work was common, as was military and quasi-military duty (the night watch).[8] Compulsion was occasionally used even to keep town offices filled; townsmen were to be fined if they balked at voluntary service in the somewhat distasteful and overburdensome office of constable. Thus compulsion in all areas of labor, even government, was common and continued to be so well into the eighteenth century.[9]

In Tudor society compulsion extended to poor relief. The ablebodied poor were compelled to work, and those too old, or otherwise incapacitated, to do so, were considered a part of the community which had to be provided a subsistence by society. Henry VIII made poor relief a compulsory obligation of the English parishes and prohibited private almsgiving.[10] Elizabethan statutes strengthened the laws, and they became a settled part of the English social system.[11] Care of the poor was not particularly generous or humane, but it was there, and no more optional than any other part of the English institutional set. Those judged to be vagabonds under the law of Henry VIII were "to be kept in continual labour." A first offense as a vagabond brought a whipping and deportation to his place of origin. On the second offense he was to have "the gristle of his right ear cut off," and if he still "doth not apply to his labour," he was to be "executed as a felon." This law was continued and amended by Elizabeth and the

---

[7]See note 2 above.

[8]*Colonial Laws of Massachusetts*, pp. 35, 160, 175-81, 198-99. Weeden (1:409) reports a Connecticut law of 1693 requiring each man to labor one day a year at clearing brush from public roadways. In 1711 Philadelphia converted compulsory road labor to a money payment of 1s. 6d. for each day's work due; in Georgia in the 1750s road work and work on bridges was assigned to the population (Allinson and Penrose, *Philadelphia*, p. 30; Jones, *History of Georgia*, 1:479). As late as the 1820s Massachusetts still used the labor tax to maintain township roads (Oscar Handlin and Mary Flug Handlin, *Commonwealth, a Study of the Role of Government in the American Economy: Massachusetts, 1774-1861* [New York, 1947], p. 48).

[9]*Colonial Laws of Massachusetts*, pp. 153, 196; Bridenbaugh, pp. 64-68, 375-78.

[10]27 Henry VIII, c. 25. The statute has no title; its first subject is "charitable alms."

[11]The Elizabethan laws were the Statute of Artificers and Apprentices and 39 Elizabeth, c 4, "An act for punishment of rogues, vagabonds and sturdy beggars."

Stuarts. Vagabond children between ages five and fourteen were to be placed as apprentices. Carl Bridenbaugh said of the early colonial practices that there was "little idea of social experimentation at first and that the laws of England were applied directly."[12] Hence one would expect to find punitive attitudes toward the unemployed, inmates of workhouses, held by the overseers of the poor in the colonies, and one did. Jefferson boasted that the poor were aided in their homes in Virginia and that "I never saw a native American begging in the streets or highways." But he also wrote, "Vagabonds, without visible property or vocation, are placed in workhouses, where they are well clothed, fed, lodged and made to labor."[13]

In 1639 the elders of Massachusetts had made similar provisions for the poor in an act empowering magistrates to "settle" the poor upon the community. Laws of 1646, 1655, and 1657 empowered magistrates "to commit Idle persons, or stubborn persons against such as have Authority over them, Runaways, common Drunkards, Pilferers, common night walkers, and wanton persons, as tending to uncleanes in speeches or actions," to houses of correction, each receiving ten lashes upon entering, and to set them to work on "hemp, flax or other materials" to earn "necessary bread and water, or other mean food." The master of the house of correction could whip and starve prisoners until they were brought to "some meet order."[14] The emphasis upon forced labor for the poor was typically English for the period, as was the notion that idleness was a crime. The background was the Tudor statutes dealing with vagabonds and sturdy beggars, and hence the colonists were not, in historical context, merely brutal.

Philadelphia had an almshouse for its poor which was also called, characteristically, the House of Employment, and its managers could commit poor orphans to apprenticeships, the boys to

---

[12]Bridenbaugh, pp. 475-76.

[13]*Notes*, p. 220. Vagabonds not incarcerated could simply be ordered out of town, and were (Kenneth Lockridge, "The Evolution of New England Society, 1630-1790," *Past and Present* 39 [1968] : 73). Bridenbaugh cites a New York ordinance of 1735 confining the poor who refused to work (p. 385).

[14]*Colonial Laws of Massachusetts*, pp. 184-85, 187; Bridenbaugh, pp. 231-38, 385, 475-78.

age twenty-one, the girls to age eighteen. Like the constables of Puritan Massachusetts townships, those designated to serve as overseers who refused the honor were fined.[15] Even the hand of charity was compulsory. The workhouse was known in South Carolina in the eighteenth century. By the 1750s the assembly of Maryland had provided an almshouse and a workhouse in each county. Insolvent debtors were sold by county courts into servitude, and church vestries were empowered to sell immoral women and their children into slavery. Trustees of almshouses were ordered to "compel" the poor to work. Governor Andros reported "all poore cared for" in 1678 in New York.[16] Generally the spirit of the laws was harsh, and the poor were not conceived of as separate from the criminal, but in the thought of the time, neither really was the workman. In fact, the workman had the added burden of religious obligation, for servants were admonished to follow the "ordinance of God" and be obedient to their masters.[17]

It is a point in favor of these American laws, however, that the main object of the English laws, from Henry VIII on, was not abandoned. The poor remained a communal responsibility, even on the frontier. If they were sold into indentured bondage or placed as apprentices, at least they were not left simply to starve. It was this minimal sense of communal responsibility that survived through the nineteenth century in such receptacles of charity as the county poor farms. The element of compulsion slowly died out, and the tradition of communal responsibility has made our more liberal policies of unemployment compensation, social security pensions, and welfare more or less acceptable to twentieth-century Americans. We were never strangers to communal responsibility; American society recognized the obligation not to let its poor starve from colonial times, when we were still English. However harsh its beginnings in Tudor England, the alternatives to poor relief were less agreeable, both to the poor and to a Christian people, which we were in the colonial era. Such aid to

[15] Allinson and Penrose, pp. 37-40, 68, 108.

[16] W. Roy Smith, *South Carolina*, p. 81; Mereness, *Maryland*, pp. 136, 403-6; Brodhead, p. 313.

[17] Edmund S. Morgan, *The Puritan Family* (New York, 1966) p. 112; all of ch. 5, "Masters and Servants," is useful on this subject. A useful recent survey of the Anglo-American tradition of poor relief is Frances Fox Diven and Richard A. Cloward, *Regulating the Poor* (New York, 1971), ch. 1.

the poor was never rational in an economic sense, then or now. Compulsory charity was, and is, a rock-bottom recognition that some values at least are not altogether commercial.

By the eighteenth century the formal English-style control in trades through guilds, or trade corporations (literally, officially sanctioned monopolies), in the seaboard cities seems to have largely taken the place of direct-control legislation. One thinks of these organizations now as peculiar labor monopolies wherein the functions of capitalist and laborer were oddly conflated. Yet they were a socially accepted way of controlling prices, wages, and quality of workmanship. Entry and apprenticeship were strictly controlled by long custom, and then, after the statute of 1562, by law. Quality control was embodied in the legal existence of the guild.[18] It was an ancient principle of the common law that persons undertaking to do a general business with the public were obliged to render to all who applied competent service, workman-like and at a reasonable charge. This obligation, or promise, was called an assumpsit, and violation of it was an offense.[19] Hence the guild, a corporate organization of masters and apprentices promising to give satisfaction for publicly supported monopoly privileges, was simply one form of nonmarket social control, and was perhaps more effective than direct legislation, since the wage bargain was bound to be mutually congenial.[20] In colonial

[18]The establishment of the guild merchant, a closed association of local tradesmen and artisans, is found in early English borough charters. For instance, the charter of Henry III to Liverpool in 1229 said: "the burgesses of the said borough shall have a gild merchant with a hanse and other privileges and trading rights by custom established as belonging to that gild, and no one who is not of that gild may trade in the said borough except with the consent of the said burgesses" (Bagley and Rowley, *Documentary History of England*, 1:84). As trade became more complex, the single guild in a town gave way to specific companies of merchants and separate craft guilds. The practices and rules were objects of statutory control, and the Elizabethan Statute of Artificers and Apprentices strengthened this control. Guild powers were upheld by English courts up to the end of the eighteenth century, and the legal position of the guilds was not abolished until 1835 (Holdsworth, *History of English Law* 1 [7th ed., 1956]: 540, 568, 2 [4th ed., 1936]: 390-91, 467-71, 4 [2d ed., 1937]: 321-407). In Boston in 1657 the right to engage in business was restricted to "admitted" inhabitants (Weeden, 1:80). This kind of restriction of entry into local economic life was typical of the general merchant guilds in the colonies (see Bridenbaugh, pp. 36-37, 43-46, 346, 358, 452).

[19]Charles K. Burdick, "The Origin of the Peculiar Duties of Public Service Companies," *Columbia Law Review* 11 (1911): 515, 523.

[20]Holdsworth, 2:467-71, 4:379-87.

America the establishment of tradesmen and mechanics in their own organizations was widespread but irregular as the area of settlement expanded and conflict arose both between the masters and local authority and between masters and their employees. As masters in the eighteenth century began to assume the differentiated function of retailer, in addition to their custom, or bespoke, work, the journeymen began to become specialized as mere employees.[21] The guilds lasted in some places, and not in others, and the idea survives in diluted form to this day in labor unions and trade associations. We still attempt to control wages, now and then, by governmental edict, and now, as in Elizabeth's time and in Massachusetts in the 1640s, such efforts are only partially effective.

Thus we are not surprised to find the Massachusetts forefathers attempting from the earliest days to set guildlike systems of control and apprenticeship going; it was the English system, and what the colonists understood. For example, a law of 1641 regarding brewing specified that "no other but good and wholsom beer be brewed at any time . . . and that no oppression or wrong be done to any in this mystery. It is ordered . . . that no person whatsoever, shall henceforth undertake the calling or worke of brewing beere for sale, but only such as are known, to have sufficient skill and knowledge in the art or mystery of brewing."[22] Leather was a major export and commercial item; so laws were passed forbidding butchers, curriers, or shoemakers from tanning. Only those trained in the mystery of tanning were to dress leather, and each town was to appoint a "searcher and viewer" to inspect wrought leather, with a reward of one-third of the resulting fine to the discoverers of violations.[23] We read of "guild merchants" and "town guilds," of requests from coopers, shoemakers, tilemakers, and hatters asking New England towns to set up "corporations" to control their crafts, of New England towns freely setting up and

[21]Saposs, in Commons, 1:44-57.

[22]*Colonial Laws of Massachusetts,* p. 126.

[23].Ibid., pp. 157, 168-70; Weeden, 1:174-75, 397-98. In Virginia even in 1780s there were controls against others than tanners doing such work (Jefferson, p. 223).

subsidizing monopoly positions in the trades;[24] and in New York, Philadelphia, and elsewhere the ancient system of master and apprentice came into existence. The list of the trades guilds that marched in New York on July 23, 1788, in support of adoption of the Federal Constitution is an eloquent testimonial of the success of this form of regulation of economic life in the colonial world.[25] Like most parts of the colonial economy, the trades had access to forced labor. A Massachusetts law of 1642 held that children and apprentices who were judged by the selectmen of each township to be insufficiently trained "in some honest Lawfull calling, labour, or imployment, either in husbandry or some other trade, profitable to themselves or the Common-wealth" could be taken away from their parents or masters and bound by the county court "with some masters for years," boys up to age twenty-one, girls to age eighteen.[26] In his more humane Charter of Liberties for Pennsylvania in 1682, William Penn advocated that all children at age twelve should be taught a trade "to the end none may be idle, but the poor may work to live and the rich, if they become poor, may not want."[27] In Pennsylvania penalties were not included for failure to comply.

This brings us to the complex subjects of the main forms of compulsion in the colonial labor contract, indentured labor and slavery. Both systems of compulsory labor were ubiquitous in the colonial economy. It is important to bear in mind that the compulsion to labor, for these two classes of workers, was very real; it was regulated and enforced by courts of law and their officers, by

[24]Weeden, 1:80-81, 175, 184, 190, 274, 309, 369, 397-98. Saposs (in Commons, 1: 37-39) gives examples of colonial favors, subsidies, and bounties to encourage useful trades. See also Bruce, *Economic History*, 2:421-39, 440-94, Wertenbaker, p. 49, and Bridenbaugh, pp. 199-200, 245, 357, on efforts to encourage crafts.

[25]Todd, *Story of City of New York*, pp. 354-56. A serious problem exists on the matter of evidence in the form of guild charters. John R. Commons found only two surviving pieces of documentary evidence on the establishment of trades guilds, the brewing and tanning guilds mentioned in the text above. Other bits and pieces indicate their existence in the older colonial towns and cities. But then the trail ends (Commons et al., *A Documentary History of American Industrial Society* [Cleveland, 1910], 3: 20-21).

[26]*Colonial Laws of Massachusetts*, p. 136.

[27]Hughes, *The Vital Few*, p. 55; see pp. 52-56 generally for discussion of relevant aspects of Penn's laws for his colony.

means that included corporal chastisement. Both forms of compulsion passed from the colonial economy straight into the federal period through the Federal Constitution. In the long and spirited debates at the Federal Convention in 1787 when the Constitution was being argued clause by clause, both systems of compulsory labor were vital in determining the numbers of delegates and the apportionment of direct taxes. The final compromise specified that population was to be counted by "adding to the whole Number of free Persons, including those bound to Service for a Term of Years, and excluding Indians not taxed, three fifths of all other Persons" (art. 1, sec. 2). Thus a Negro slave was counted as three-fifths of a person, an indentured servant as a whole person; Indians not settled in the states were not counted. This legacy of the colonial economy was destined to be the most difficult problem the federal republic faced, and still faces. Indenture wilted away with the years as the growth of a free labor force by immigration and natural increase made wages competitive with indenture costs. As imprisonment for debt vanished, so did the ability to enforce indentures.[28] Slavery itself was ended only by war, and its aftermath still haunts American life. The tradition of compulsory labor in the colonial economy, the practice of a mutually binding free contract inherited with the common law, and the anomalous position in the law of labor as property no doubt underlay the inability of Americans to cope with organized labor within the system of American capitalism, despite a century and a half of organized union agitation, until unions finally were established by federal legislation in the National Labor Relations Act of 1935.

Whereas we know something of the quantities involved in Negro slavery—the slaves could be counted—the numbers of persons "bound for service for a term of years," as the Constitution puts it, may well never be known. Contracts of indenture were legal documents, but to what extent they were ever recorded by legal authority is unknown. Possibly a survey of all the existing court records from 1607 onwards would produce some believable estimates of the numbers of native-born persons who passed into this form of servitude. But the contracts of immigrants coming in were

[28]Louis Hartz, *Economic Policy and Democratic Thought: Pennsylvania, 1776-1860* (Cambridge, Mass., 1948), p. 186.

sold by shipmasters and contracting merchants to buyers, commonly at the docks, and although the servants were supposed to be registered with the courts in the colonies, there is no way of knowing the extent to which such registrations were proportional to the totals. It is commonly said that about half of all white immigrants to the colonies before 1776 were bound in one way or another. Abbot E. Smith, in his exhaustive effort *Colonists in Bondage,* concluded, "If we exclude the Puritan migrations of the 1630s, it is safe to say that not less than one-half, nor more than two-thirds, of all white immigrants to the colonies were indentured servants, or redemptioners or convicts."[29]

We have already dealt with certain connections between indentured labor and economic development in the case of headright land grants. The indenture was doubtless a most feasible solution of a score of problems, including the need of a ready method to obtain land. The colonies needed people, and the mother country had an excess, especially after the statute of Elizabeth imposed a rigid structure on the growth of the English labor force. The effect of indentures upon wages must have been to lower them, since the indentured servants could not withhold their labor. On the other hand, the price of each servant did reflect local demand as well as the cost of transport, since there was apparently no effort to control the prices of indenture contracts. The sale of indenture contracts enabled middlemen, the brokers of the system, to pay the costs of transportation at, usually, a handsome return.[30] The servant, he or she hoped, was bettering his condition of life in the bargain.

The usual contract of indenture was a simple agreement in which the seller agreed to labor for a stipulated term of years at specified work in return for transport, clothing, food, housing, perhaps some fixed annual wage, and sometimes for some terminal reward at the end of the contract.[31] The last item was not mandatory; we have seen that in early Virginia some freed servants were

---

[29] *Colonists in Bondage: White Servitude and Convict Labor in America, 1607-1776* (Chapel Hill, N.C., 1947), p. 336; see also p. 307.

[30] Ibid., p. 39; see also Bruce, *Economic History,* 2:1 n.1.

[31] A. E. Smith, pp. 16-17. An example of a seven-year indenture contract is given in Kingsbury, *Records of Virginia Company,* 3:314. See also Morgan, *The Puritan Family,* pp. 120-21, and "The First American Boom," pp. 176, 184.

provided with land and others were not. In the Massachusetts laws of 1641 it was loosely provided that "servants that have served deligentie and faithfully to the benefitt of their maisters seaven yeares, shall not be sent away empty." Nothing specific was suggested as reward, but unsatisfactory service was explicitly threatened with extended terms "according to the Judgement of Authoritie."[32] Penn, on the other hand, set aside a portion of his lands explicitly for indentured servants who had served their terms, with the usual conditions attached, including quitrents.[33] In most of the other colonies land was easy enough to come by, and servants sufficiently desirable, that provision was also made for servants to acquire lands at the end of their indentures, but usually without any preference regarding conditions.[34] There seems to have been no set number of years for indentures to run, except they seem mainly to have fallen between three and seven years, depending on circumstances. In early Virginia children were in great demand as they could be held longest in service. The Virginia Company bought them in London at £5 a head, and in 1627 alone between 1,400 and 1,500 children were shipped to Virginia. The impetus for free persons to indenture themselves was clearly dire poverty. The profitability in their transport was measured by opportunity cost, the difference between the profit on selling and transporting servants as against other goods. This margin of profit seems to have been high.[35]

Redemptioners were not quite the same as indentured servants; they were not just human merchandise. They arrived at colonial ports technically free, but owing the shipmaster for passage. They then had some short period of time to arrange for payment by work, perhaps putting one or more children into indentures to pay the passage money.[36] The system is thought to have begun with the German immigration to the colonies at the middle of the eighteenth century. Convicts, on the other hand, were merchandise. Transportation of convicts was a notorious sore point in the

[32]*Colonial Laws of Massachusetts*, p. 53.   [33]Hughes, p. 54.

[34]Mereness, p. 134; Jones, p. 109.

[35]Bruce, *Economic History*, 1:593-94; A. E. Smith, pp. 39-41, ch. 11; Morgan, "The First American Boom," throughout, on demand for servants in Virginia.

[36]A. E. Smith, p. 22.

colonies. Rogues and vagabonds, as defined in an Elizabethan statute, could be transported, and were, until that statute was repealed in 1713.[37] In the seventeenth century some three hundred crimes in England carried the death penalty, but many felonies were clergyable (subject to benefit of clergy), or commutable, and the felons could be pardoned from the gallows on condition that they transport themselves to the colonies. Nonclergyable felonies could also be pardoned on condition of transportation. Convicts transported by these means were nearly always on seven years' indentures; hence arose the phrase describing so many thousands of our ancestors as "His Majesty's Seven-Year Passengers." Once the king had signed the pardons, the whole system became a strictly private operation. There were regular convict merchants who gathered their passengers from the sheriffs and the Recorder of London or bribed jailers and turnkeys. Convict contractors made regular circuits of the English court system gathering their merchandise. Efforts by the colonies to stop the shipping of convicts failed, and it is recorded that in 1783, after the Revolution, at least one convict transport arrived from England in the United States. In 1788 Congress passed a resolution against receiving further English "gaol deliveries" in this country, and the English began looking to Australia.[38] Perhaps 4,500 convicts were shipped from 1661 to 1700 and perhaps 30,000 from 1700 to 1776.[39] A minor, though much-heralded, source of convict manpower was political defeat. After the battles of Preston and Worcester thousands of Scottish prisoners were shipped, and many more after the Jacobite risings in 1715 and 1745. Irish prisoners were shipped by

[37]Ibid., pp. 136-317; 39 Elizabeth, c. 4.

[38]A. E. Smith, pp. 90-116, 119-21, 123-24.

[39]Ibid., pp. 96, 116. The system was used periodically to clear up London vice and simultaneously to supply female prisoners for the settlements. A. E. Smith quotes a report of the Venetian ambassador in 1655 that "the soldiers of the London Garrison had visited various brothels and other places of entertainment and forcibly laid hands on more than four hundred women of loose life, whom they compelled to sail for the Barbados Islands" (pp. 142-43). The same technique was used in 1787 to settle 60 white women "of abandoned character" with 400 freed American slaves in Sierra Leone. The slaves had been freed by British troops during the American Revolution, and Sierra Leone was settled as a solution to the problem of finding them a home (*Cambridge History of the British Empire*, vol. 2 [Cambridge, 1961], pp. 208-12).

William of Orange in 1690. Some of the duke of Monmouth's soldiers had also been shipped in 1685. Similarly, many of the
French Candians from Acadia, now Nova Scotia, were sent as
bonded servants to the southern colonies in 1755. The military
prisoners were as welcome as the others. John Cotton wrote from
Boston to Cromwell on May 25, 1651: "The Scots, whom God
delivered into your hands at Dunbarre, and whereof sundry were
sent hither, we have been desirous (as we could) to make their
yoke easy. Such as were sick of scurvy or other diseases have not
wanted physick and Chryurgery. They have not been sold for
slaves to perpetuall servitude, but for 6 or 7 or 8 years, as we do
our owne; and he that bought the most of them (I heare) buildeth
houses for them, for every 4 an house, layeth some acres of
ground thereto, which he giveth them as their owne, requiering 3
dayes in the weeke to worke for him (by turnes) and 4 dayes for
themselves, and promiseth, assone as they can repay him the
money he layed out for them, he will set them at liberty."[40]

All these persons had little more choice of occupation during
their indentures than did slaves and doubtless usually continued
after their freedom to pursue the skills they had learned as servants. As those skills were likely, in the circumstances, to be precisely the ones most needed by the colonists, this large-scale and
long-term injection of labor into the colonial economy may be
considered as socially directed. In fact, it is difficult to imagine
how it could have been more so. If one assumes that at least the
planters knew best where lay the highest returns to labor and
capital within the existing alternatives, the power to employ fixed-
cost labor arbitrarily must have offered a unique prospect for
maximum economic efficiency. It is also difficult to believe that
without compulsion a substitute free labor force would have come
across the ocean, except for the religious schismatics, and even
they liberally indulged in both slaves and indentured servants. In
fact, they sold their own debtors into servitude, and Massachusetts
passed a law to keep persons from selling themselves into servitude
to avoid obligations to pay off their creditors.[41] It must be concluded that indentured labor was cheaper, that is, more productive, than free labor, as was also the case with Negro slavery.

[40]*Hutchinson Papers,* 1:264. See also Bruce, *Economic History,* 1:608-9.

[41]Weeden, 1: 275; Bridenbaugh, pp. 46-48.

Although the introduction and maintenance of both systems have often been blamed on the British by American historians, it is significant that neither system ceased in 1776. The southern defenses of the "peculiar institution" are well known. Jefferson, for example, stated the common belief that "in a warm climate, no man will labour for himself who can make another labour for him."[42] Perhaps none was less rational than the resolution passed by the Pennsylvania assembly in 1778 as a reaction against the suggestion that indentured servants should be made free: "Resolved that all Apprentices and servants are the property of their masters and mistresses, and every mode of depriving such masters and mistresses of their Property is a Violation of the Rights of mankind."[43]

The history of Negro slavery is well known and need not be treated extensively here. Given the extent of control over labor and work in all other parts of the colonial economy, though, one can see that the Negro slaves were not the only persons laboring in conditions of total servitude. It is just that the conditions of their servitude were so much worse than those of white bondsmen and bondswomen—see any of the various colonial slave codes—and offered little chance of freedom to parents or to children. Most students of this grim subject agree that American slavery was in a class by itself when it came to inhumane treatment—not necessarily brutality, just the denial that the Negro was, at least in law, a human being at all. In any case, Negro slavery was another facet, and a large one, of a colonial labor system rooted in compulsion.

At the end of the colonial period, in 1780, there were over 575,000 Negroes in a total American population of just under 2.8 million, or about 20 percent of the total. Virginia had 220,600, South Carolina, 97,000, North Carolina, 91,000, Maryland, 81,000, Georgia 20,800, and somewhat surprisingly, New York,

---

[42]Pp. 271-72.   [43]A. E. Smith, pp. 283-84.

[44]*Historical Statistics of the United States* (Washington, D.C., 1958), tables Z-19, Z-20. For a survey of colonial slave data, including the entire Atlantic slave trade, see Robert Fogel and Stanley Engerman, *Time on the Cross: The Economics of American Negro Slavery* (Boston, 1974), ch. 1, and *Time on the Cross: Evidence and Methods—A Supplement* (Boston, 1974), notes to ch. 1, pp. 27-37. Fogel and Engerman are concerned mainly with American slavery after the American Revolution. Their arguments about the Negro slave "contract" mainly agree with my own in what follows, except that

21,000; the New England colonies had the fewest slaves, in total and proportionally.[44] Each colony had some slaves; slavery, like bonded servitude among whites, was ubiquitous, and had been from early times, even in New England.[45] The concentration of the Negroes in the southern colonies represented the economic reality of the system. Most of the imported slaves had gone to those colonies, and since the child followed his mother's condition, most of the natural increase had remained southern slaves. Decade after decade throughout the colonial period the slaves were imported, and the seaport cities added the open market in black flesh to the servitude of the whites in the creation of a labor force of the unfree.

Economically, slavery had distinct advantages over indentured labor if conditions were right.[46] From contemporary accounts it is clear that the colonial planters and proprietors in the main southern colonies believed that Negro slavery was the cheapest solution to the problems of plantation agriculture, and acted accordingly. But the numbers of blacks in colonies like New York, New Jersey (10,500), Pennsylvania (7,900), Connecticut (5,900), and Massachusetts (4,800) in 1780 indicate that slavery was competitive in some uses with free or indentured white servants and workers.[47] In plantation agriculture, however, where gang

---

I emphasize the elements of compulsion, together with the subsidy to slave owners implied in communal enforcement of the slave codes.

[45]*Colonial Laws of Massachusetts*, p. 53. The original Liberties of 1641, no. 91, stated: "There shall never be any bond slavery, villinage or Captivities amongst us unles it be lawfull Captives taken in just Warres, and such strangers as willingly selle themselves or are sold to us." These exceptions were sufficient. See Channing, *History of U.S.*, 2: 383-84.

[46]It has long been understood that plantation slavery in the American South was a profitable business, despite many disclaimers. Since 1958, beginning with a celebrated paper by Alfred Conrad and John Meyer, the profitability of slavery has been the subject of extensive research. Fogel and Engerman reprinted the major papers with some additional contributions of their own in *The Reinterpretation of American Economic History* (New York, 1971), pt. 7. For a description of the slave laws and their psychological impact, see Stanley Elkins, *Slavery* (New York, 1963), pp. 81-139. Fogel and Engerman have now reexamined the entire issue in *Time on the Cross* on a scale not likely to be duplicated. They still find plantation slavery to have been a profitable business.

[47]*Historical Statistics of U.S.*, table Z-20; Fogel and Engerman, *Time on the Cross*, pp. 44-52.

labor was employed under supervision, the costs of management were spread over enough productive units to yield scale economies even if it could be argued that physical compulsion might have been less effective than monetary rewards, had such been offered. The wage (food, clothing, shelter) of the slave could be arbitrarily controlled more easily than that of indentured labor, which had effective access to the courts for violations of contract.[48] Moreover, the direct costs of management and the policing of the slave force were subsidized outright by the community. The stringent slave laws[49] and their brutal enforcement, severely limiting the education, social lives, and training of slaves, meant that the community as a whole taxed itself to support the slave owner. Doubtless the motivation was fear and self defense, but the economic result was a subsidy. In addition, headright lands were granted equally for transporting slaves or servants. Thus in the economics of the land distribution system employed, in the South, money spent on the slave was also land acquisition. The slave's contract was for life rather than for a limited term of years, so the transaction costs were therefore lower per unit of labor; transportation costs were reduced for the buyer to a single ocean voyage per life of the labor unit. If a slave lived twenty-one years in an area where the normal indenture was seven years, the transport cost of one slave was at the minimum only a third of the alternative, the transport costs for three indentured servants. There was also little termination cost for a slave beyond the cost of burying him, since his contract was for life, whereas indentured servants usually were allotted a stock of food, goods, and tools at the end of their contracts. Because servants also commonly had to be educated or trained during their indentures according to their contracts, they were more expensive to maintain on a current basis even if no better clothed or fed than slaves. Finally, the female slave was a prime capital asset, as her offspring, either from a white or a black father, added to the slave stock, and this was not true of indentured females. This fact alone must have been a heavy incentive to use slaves. That the slave tended to be capitalized—used up economically—before his biological life was over and had to be supported by the slave owner during his declining years was an

[48] A. E. Smith, ch. 12; Morgan, "The First American Boom," p. 195.

[49] Jones, 1:479-83; Bruce, *Economic History*, 2:108-22; Channing, 2:375-78.

economic curiosity of the system, but obviously the cost was small enough not to offset the other economic advantages of slavery.

Not the least of these was the dependability of overseas supply during the colonial era. The British people subsidized the supply through taxation, since government sponsorship itself either was for long the major source of the supply of slaves or, as in later years, protected with warships and all the powers of state the independent slavers operating out of Britain and the colonies. Attempts to maintain official monopolies in the trade lasted from 1631 to 1698. In that year the trade was partly opened to private slavers on payment of a tax to the crown on "African goods" exported from England. The crown monopoly, the Royal Africa Company, also continued. In 1713, under the Treaty of Utrecht, a grant from the Spanish crown, the asiento, opened the whole of Spanish America to English slavers. Both the English and Spanish governments granted outright subsidies to the trade. In 1750 the Royal Africa Company went bankrupt, ending English efforts to maintain even the semblance of monopoly in the trade, and it was thrown open to private entrepreneurs on condition of payment of taxes on trade goods. Shipments boomed. Royal governors in the colonies were regularly instructed to foster the trade, and equally regularly the crown disallowed the periodic laws passed by the colonies to stop the trade or limit it. The whole weight of the central government stood behind the supply of slaves,[50] and it was steady and abundant. The crown's interested was fixed early in the eighteenth century by Chief Justice Holt's dictum that "negroes are merchandise and within the Navigation acts."[51] But by the end of that century most of the increment in slave population was natural increase.

Both sides of the market, demand and supply, thus contained elements favorable to the growth of the slave system as a means of supplying labor, just as the laws of England and the needs and customs of the colonists accounted for the thriving system of indentured labor. This colonial labor system based on compulsion of varying degrees of crudity was firmly rooted. As Abbot E.

[50]W. E. B. Dubois, *The Suppression of the African Slave Trade to the United States of America* (Cambridge, Mass., 1896), pp. 1-6; Channing, pp. 395-98.

[51]McCrady, *History of South Carolina*, p. 385; Andrews, *Colonial Period*, 4:83 n.3.

Smith put it, "Colonial society was not democratic, and certainly not equalitarian; it was dominated by men who had money enough to make others work for them."[52]

The sale of men, women, and children for life or for terms of years, off ships or out of slave pens, prisons, poorhouses, and jails, was as common in colonial life as public hangings and floggings. It was a harsh era. Slave prices varied according to the qualities of the persons for sale and market conditions, just as the prices for indentured servants did, except that the latter tended to vary with the time their contracts had to run. Servitude was not only a solution for debtors and orphans but also a common punishment for crimes, combined often with public entertainment. For example, Ezra Stiles, future president of Yale, noted in his diary on September 24, 1771, that "judg[ment] was given upon Pond for Theft . . . to pay £150 . . . Damages to Mr. Pease, £100 fine, stand in the pillory with a rope round his neck for two hours, & be whipped 39 stripes, & sold for not exceeding the Term of seven years."[53] A slave might be sold also for a term of years, and ultimately become a free man, if so contracted. For example, from Virginia records in the late seventeenth century the following sale of a slave was made from a New England ship: "Know all men by these presents that I John Endicott, Cooper, of Boston in New England, have sold unto Richard Medlicott, a Spanish Mulatto, by name Antonio, I having full power to sell for his life time, but at ye request of William Taylor, I do sell him but for ten years from ye day that he shall disembark for Virginia . . . and at ye expiration of ye said ten years, ye said Mulatto to be a free man to go wheresoever he pleases."[54] The term of years for such slave sales varied widely, but slavery for life was, of course, by far the most favored mode. Moreover, freed slaves were common; there were cases of headright grants given former slaves upon their importation of other slaves, and in one known case a former slave received a headright grant of 100 acres for the importation of two white indentured servants.[55]

The law establishing Negro slavery was not questioned, nor was the system of indenture in colonial times. Regulation and moral

---

[52]P. 7. [53]*Literary Diary*, p. 165.
[54]Bruce, *Economic History*, 2:81 n.2. [55]Ibid., p. 126.

objection were another matter. All the colonies taxed slave imports for revenue in varying degrees, and in some cases the object of taxation was explicitly to discourage or regulate imports. But the shippers and merchants of the northern colonies, especially Massachusetts and Rhode Island, were massively engaged in the slave trade by the mid-eighteenth century, and whatever moral scruples existed against this practice were generally kept under control.[56] In New York from 1665 to 1683, under the Duke's Laws, it was illegal for a Christian to own a slave who served unwillingly.[57] But by 1740 the legislature declared that the importation of Negro slaves should be encouraged, and it condemned smuggling as "an eminent discouragement to fair trade."[58] The New England colonies from time to time expressed unhappiness with the importation of black slaves into their territories, but they were engaged in the profitable triangular trade of rum, slaves, and sugar with Africa and the West Indies and were in no economic position to take a strong moral stand. Their colonial laws, masterfully summarized by W. E. B. Dubois, illustrate a hopeless compromise between morals and money, so that little Rhode Island was not only an early leader in the abolition movement but the most extensive slave shipper of all.[59] From the first organized statement against Negro slavery in 1688, by the Germantown, Pennsylvania, Quakers, down to Jefferson's lament in his *Notes on Virginia* that "I tremble for my country, when I reflect that God is just; that his justice cannot sleep forever," the hypocrisy of American whites and Negro slavery makes sad reading. The system was too deeply rooted to be easily abolished. A slave was property, like real estate, could be rented out, could be freely aliened, could be entailed, passed as widow's dower, devised, or inherited when the owner died intestate.[60] An indentured servant's contract ended with the death of his master. The difference was immense, and yet even indenture lived on in American history.

[56]Dubois, pp. 27-29 and, generally, chs. 2, 3, and 4.

[57]Channing, 2:387. Dubois thought the New York law of no real consequence (p. 18).

[58]Kent, *Commentaries*, 2:255.   [59]Dubois, pp. 33-36.

[60]Jefferson, pp. 228-30; Kent, 2:305-18; Bruce, *Economic History*, 2:98.

So from the Spanish importation of Negroes to the Caribbean in 1501, the first landing of slaves in Virginia in 1619, down to the eve of the Revolution, the system thrived. One of history's "might-have-beens" was lost to America by the Revolution. In London, in 1772, a Negro slave named Somerset was freed by the court on a writ of habeas corpus; in the opinion of Lord Mansfield, the great jurist who presided, slavery did not exist in the English constitution, and no man thereafter touching upon the soil of England was a slave.[61] By a long and tortuous route Britain led the suppression of the slave trade and finally, in 1834, freed the slaves in the British Caribbean by compensated emancipation. It is hard to imagine that Negro slavery would have continued in the American colonies had they remained British, for their laws could not have continued to be "repugnant to the laws of this our realm of England."

As it was, there was a concerted move to eliminate the slave trade and then slavery itself in the northern colonies on the eve of the Revolution and more decidedly after independence. But the men who wrote the Federal Constitution compromised with their southern colleagues on the issue, agreeing that slavery was a matter of "interest" and not morals,[62] and slavery as well as bonded indenture passed into modern American history. The labor system of the new republic began its existence stained by the colonial past. As Abbot E. Smith said of this part of the American tradition: "It is a familiar story that mankind, when confronted in America with a vast and trackless wilderness awaiting exploitation, threw off its ancient shackles of cast and privilege and set forth upon the road to freedom. Among the social institutions found most useful in the course of this march were those of African slavery and white servitude."[63]

Unlike white servitude, Negro slavery gave rise to a racial discrimination which outlived the unfree labor system. Laws against intermarriage continued until our own time, along with segregation and general intolerance. The terrible laws imposed upon

---

[61]Kent, 2:306; McCrady, pp. 381-85.

[62]*Documents Illustrative of the Formation of the Union*, p. 588.

[63]P. 226.

African slaves in colonial times and their barbaric enforcement—
including public dismemberments and crucifixions—are agrument
enough against those who believe that American racial discrimination is somehow a consequence of the Civil War. This historical
root was far deeper, and virtually all of colonial America was
implicated in it. The whole colonial labor system was harsh and
brutal. But it was Negro slavery, and not the infinity of other
servitudes endured by men and women of all races who worked
with their hands, whose scars time has not healed. The forces of
economic pressures that liberated the landowner from the incidents of feudal tenure, and, as we shall see, broke down the main
constraints against commerce, worked only slowly to liberate
white labor from the fetters of the medieval past, and did not
work to emancipate the Negro. In economic terms the reasons
seem simple: slaves were real property, and slavery paid. Such was
the tenor of the discussion at the Constitutional Convention when
in 1787 the slave trade itself was granted another twenty years of
life in exchange for southern votes, and such was the system that
was finally destroyed by military violence when the Union was
ripped apart by the slave question. As Dubois put it at the end of
his great study: "With the faith of the nation broken at the very
outset, the system of slavery untouched, and twenty years' respite
given to the slave trade to feed and foster it, there began, with
1787, that system of bargaining, truckling, and compromising with
a moral, political, and ecocomic monstrosity, which makes the
history of our dealing with slavery in the first half of the nineteenth century so discreditable to a great people."[64]

The labor system has been one part of the colonial heritage that
historians have wisely left largely uncelebrated. It did, however,
exist and had incalculable long-range consequences, celebrated or
not. Economically, judging from the growth of the colonial economy, it was relatively efficient. To explain the labor system's lack
of change, the Elizabethan beginning may be cited. The land
tenure system imported from England was one which could not go
backwards toward the constraints of feudalism because socage was

---

[64]P. 198. There were, of course, eloquent moral arguments made against slavery; see
Madison's record of the convention's debates in *Documents Illustrative of the Formation
of the Union*, pp. 495-98, 589.

nonmilitary, and increasing freedom of land ownership was a logical development on the frontier. But the Statute of Artificers and Apprentices was basically static and medieval in conception, and movement toward a freer labor contract ran up against a strong institutional barrier and its long-run social effects in terms of attitudes toward labor and working people. It is therefore not surprising that growth of a free labor contract and an equal wage bargain came in America only long after the constraints of the old land tenure and property system had mostly disappeared. Land was abundant; labor was not. An economic system which worked only to conserve the scarce factor might logically limit the freedom of labor where coercion was possible. But the availability of the land mitigated this action to a large extent among whites, who could not be forced to accept the wage bargain. Relatively high wages and, ultimately, even labor unions resulted. The case of the Negro slave before 1865 was different. Most slaves had no alternative to their bondage before the Civil War, and racial discrimination limited all Negroes' access to jobs and unions afterward, even to this writing.

9

Nonmarket Control
and the Price Nexus

In view of the primitive nature of the early settlements, together with the many decades it took in the seventeenth century for the customary amenities of town and commercial life to appear, the evidence of well-ordered and sophisticated procedures in business transactions is perhaps justifiably surprising. It seems paradoxical that deeds, contracts, sales, and leases should have been so punctiliously arranged among a people who for long decades were forced to maintain a commercial life only barely above the level of barter. The early colonists, with hardly the rudiments of domestic production beyond agriculture, firmly enacted laws controlling the qualities and prices of such goods as were produced. A people having no banks and using corn, tobacco, beaver skins, and wampum for currency passed laws controlling interest rates, carefully arranged the amortization of their own instruments of credit, and rigorously enforced the transfer of negotiable instruments and the rules for payment of debt. Similarly, despite appalling mortality rates and only the beginnings of an organized land market, they meticulously worked out the laws of alienation and descent of land. Leases and rentals were utilized with facility. Partnerships and joint ownerships of all sorts appeared, as did such things as public franchises and subsidies.[1] These were but a part of the vast and intangible thing historians call the English heritage which enabled colonial economic development at the level of private

[1] Even the special franchise monopoly with subsidy added appeared early. For example, in Massachusetts in 1641 it was provided that "no monopolies shall be granted or allowed amongst us"; yet in 1644 it was resolved "that for the better building of shipping within this judisdiction, and for avoiding of many inconveniences which both owners and builders are subject unto, there be a company of that trade, according to the manner of other places, with power to regulate building of ships." In 1668 a monopoly was offered for anyone willing to build a dock in Boston (*Colonial Laws of Massachusetts*, pp. 35, 72, 244). In New York in 1675 a special corporation was chartered "for settling a fishery in these parts" (Brodhead, *History of State of New York*, 1:276).

business to occur with little friction. This intellectual technology was available should opportunity to use it arise, and it ultimately did.

One easily overlooks these things because they were both complex and unseen. They came over in the minds of the colonists. They cannot be counted and analyzed quantitatively, yet their presence certainly was necessary for the kind of economic growth that occurred, for this basic framework of commercial life gave the colonists flexible administrative rules of conduct which put them on a par with their English cousins, who were already, in the seventeenth century, assuming the economic leadership of Europe on the basis of their ways of conducting commercial life. When the time came to erect factories, build and operate ships on shares, insure both cargoes and hulls, ultimately to coin and print money and form complicated commercial organizations, the colonists could act with the natural ease that came from everyday familiarity with business. Their period as an underdeveloped nation, in the modern parlance, was short. They were equipped intellectually to come abreast of the commercial world when they could command the necessary physical resources. Hence they were unlike modern underdeveloped nations.[2] The colonists were, in business as in politics, at least the equals of their British competitors who operated out of the mother country. The consequences were profound and doubtless contributed as much as did any other forces to produce the cleavage between the colonial and British economies that came in the American Revolution. In the case of the American colonies dependency upon the mother country finally had to be enforced; by the mid-eighteenth century it was not the natural thing it had been, temporarily, in earlier times.

As with the basic framework governing the conditions of labor, the English institutional system governing business appeared in

---

[2]For example, the colonists very early tried to provide for schools, however irregularly, in New England by township and elsewhere by town, county, or church. One can but be moved, even now, to find in the Massachusetts laws of 1636, 1640, and 1642 provisions for Harvard: a grant of £400 and the revenues of the ferry between Charlestown and Boston (*Colonial Laws of Massachusetts*, p. 138). The general establishment of the infrastructure of a commercial world is described in Bridenbaugh, *Cities in the Wilderness*.

America at first largely intact. This was natural enough; one does what one knows how to do. What the colonists knew how to do in business was based upon the English law of contract, of sale, and alienation, and of franchise. There was, as now, an infinity of possible permutations.

The basic foundation of business transactions is the contract itself. The colonial charters were contracts, as we have noted. Feudal land tenures were contracts, marriages were contracts, obligations of tradesmen and laborers were contracts. The idea of contract permeates English history. The sanctity of contract in England lay at the very root of the developing idea of government by law and not by men. Blackstone said of the power of contract in the common law: "a contract for any *valuable* consideration, as for marriage, for money, for work done, or for reciprocal contracts, can never be impeached at law; and, if it be of sufficient adequate value, is never set aside in equity."[3]

When the contract clause (art. 1, sec. 10) of the Federal Constitution was written, forbidding the states to pass laws infringing contracts, the common law was being legislated for the new republic. Lord Coke had argued against even the rights of king and Parliament to legislate against the common law,[4] and in its clause the Constitutional Convention laid such a constraint against the states in regard to contract. The idea of contract was, after all, imbedded in the colonial charters, in all the grants of land, in sales and wills, and in all business dealings. It was the power of contract, as we have seen, that enabled something as basically "un-American" as the feudal encumbrances of the land tenures and leases in the manor counties of New York to exist as late as the mid-nineteenth century and apprenticeship even longer.[5] Even the

---

[3] *Commentaries*, bk. 2, p. 359.

[4] Pound, "Development of American Law and Its Deviation from English Law," pp. 58-59.

[5] Indentured servants, like criminals under the ancient English law of hue and cry, were ordered to be delivered up upon demand in the Constitution, art. 4, sec. 2: "No person held to Service of Labour in one State. . . ." This provision led to the Civil War via the Dred Scott decision. In the previous paragraph of this section, "A Person charged in any State with Treason, felony or other crime . . .," is in fact the American version of Edward I's Statute of Winchester of 1285.

contractual power of the holder in due course of a financial instrument, that is, someone other than the first owner, a fairly arcane application, appeared early. The common bank check of today is a bill of exchange, an order to pay, and a negotiable instrument. Title is passed by signature, and the final holder has all the rights of the first holder. In 1647 the colonial laws of Massachusetts were amended to read: "any debt, or debts due upon bill or other specialty assigned to another, shall be as good a debt & estate to the Assignee, as it was to the assigner, at the time of its assignation; And that it shall be lawful for the said Assignee, to sue for, & recover the said debt due upon bills, & so assigned, as fully as the original creditor might have done; provided the sayd assignment be made upon the back-side of the bill or specialtie."[6]

These laws also provided for defenses against fraud.[7] The law could hardly be more modern; in its logical ramifications it contained the whole corpus of the laws of negotiable instruments, so necessary for credit to be created and mobilized in the interests of economic development. Debt could be created, transferred, and collected. The Massachusetts Puritans were so sophisticated in these matters that in 1654 they stipulated a "gold clause" in the construction of contracts for payment in kind. A people forced to use goods for money, they knew that relative scarcities might change with hunting, fishing, or harvest conditions. Both the buyer and the seller were held to the original bargain: "all *contracts* and *engagements,* for *money, corn, cattle,* or *fish,* shall be satisfied in kind according to Covenant, or in default of the very kind contracted for, in one of the said kinds, Provided that in such cases, where payment in kind is not made according to covenant; all just damage shall be satisfied . . . according to bargain."[8]

In cases where goods were seized, distrained, or held in distress for debt, the Massachusetts laws were a portent of later state laws protecting the debtor from the wastage of his impounded property.[9] Seizures of chattels, or movable, personal property, for debt

---

[6]*Colonial Laws of Massachusetts,* p. 125.   [7]Ibid., pp. 37, 39, 43, 140-41.
[8]Ibid., p. 183.   [9]Kent, *Commentaries,* 3:619-46, 4:443-61.

had been provided for in Magna Carta.[10] But the Puritans had an eye on the fact that it was the debtor in a frontier community who was likely to be the cutting edge of civilization. The creditor had to be supported in his contract rights, but if goods seized and held by legal authorities as surety against payment of debts deteriorated while impounded, there was, paradoxically, a confiscation of the debtor's property. Livestock and ripened crops in the field must be protected. The Body of Liberties of 1641 declared that nothing perishable could be taken in distress for debt "unles he that takes it doth presently bestow it where it may not be imbesled nor suffer spoil or decay, or give security to satisfie the worth thereof if it comes to any harme." Logically, domestic capital equipment should also be protected, so an addition to the law in 1647 stated that in execution for debt legal authorities could not take "any mans necessary bedding, apparrel, tools or armes, neither implements or house-hold, which are for the necessary upholding of his life."[11] Such a construction of the law became general in the colonies, and in the federal period was reflected in the state laws, with the exception of Louisiana, where an artisan's tools could be seized.[12] Louisiana's laws had a different origin, of course. Since enforcement of rent contracts originally descended from feudal tenures, the position of the renter in case of nonpayment was particularly weak, and the strengthening of the debtor's position in colonial and early state laws was simply recognition of the de facto shift of power in the community away from hereditary landlords.

The law similarly bent when land was seized for debt. Such a seizure was an extraordinary occurrence in England,[13] and in fact made little sense in its law, for a seizure would break the feudal chain of property right. The usual procedure there was for the court to grant all or a portion of the annual yield of land to the landholder's creditor. But eventually in 1731 Parliament passed a law subjecting American land to seizure and sale for debt as if it were chattel goods. This became general colonial law except in

---

[10]Magna Carta, art. 9, in Bagley and Rowley, *Documentary History of England,* p. 102.

[11]*Colonial Laws of Massachusetts,* pp. 41, 174.   [12]Kent, 3:637 n.(b).

[13]Magna Carta, art 9, in Bagley and Rowley, p. 102; Kent, 4:443.

Virginia.[14] Since land was in fact becoming a pure commodity in America, having a real existence unencumbered by the developing commercial and social system of the colonies, such a transformation of land law made sense in connection with the law of contract, and much earlier in some of the colonies, beginning in 1696 with Massachusetts (where land was least encumbered by feudal incidents), land had been seized and sold for debt as if it were chattels. However, it became the custom for the improved part of the land to be treated as "tools"; it, and the homesite, were seized only if the unimproved land failed to satisfy the debt.[15] This custom is an excellent example of law's bending to meet both a new reality—land as a commodity—and a pressing social need—maximum encouragement for pioneer families. Oddly, we got that law from the English—through Parliament's action—but not from English law. The English law of contract prevailed in the colonial setting, but not without a subtle change which matched the needs of settlement. On the other hand, in later years, as we noted earlier, efforts by the states under the stop laws to force land upon creditors at locally fixed rates were struck down by the courts; the law was not perfectly flexible to the needs of pioneering. The long-run consequences of land seizure for debt, together with the states' stepping in after the Revolution as the ultimate fee holders in escheatment for nonpayment of taxes, remain to this day. American landowners hold only for good behavior—as long as they pay their taxes and their private debts, including mortgages.

Looking back at the colonies there are few subjects more obscure and yet fundamental to economic development than the emergence of markets for domestically produced commodities. On this single point, the transference of ownership of chattels by sale, is concentrated a host of nonmarket social control mechanisms transplanted from England. From it, with the passage of time and the growth of the massive internal market, came a good deal of our precedent for such burning contemporary issues as consumer protection, price controls, fraudulent conveyance, and all the domestic concerns which burden municipal law and federal

---

[14]Kent, 4:443-44. The law was 5 George II, C. 7.

[15]Kent, 4:444, 445 n.(b). This is the origin of the "homestead exemption" that still prevails in many states.

legislation and regulation alike. Here, as with land ownership, the traditions and place of labor in the economy, and the dominion of contract, modern problems and practice are rooted in a distant past.

When the colonists had created an economy beyond the initial landings and the communal efforts required for survival itself, it was necessary to specialize and trade. At this point three parts of the English tradition came together and were at first inseparable: (1) under what conditions domestic trade might occur, (2) what title in goods could pass in trade, and (3) what goods could be traded. These three items embrace the whole world of economic change and development that transformed colonial America into the nineteenth-century economy, and left its traces upon economic life today.

At first the historical record on these matters is fairly mysterious. Certain controls are immediately recognizable as the regulation of franchises and public utilities. Innkeepers, common carriers, and persons with special monopolies to operate ferries and toll bridges were placed under strict regulation from the time of the earliest colonial laws. Since such nonmarket social controls still exist (now magnified enormously), these laws are familiar and congenial to our understanding. The laws which are strange now relate to controls over places and times at which goods could be offered publicly for sale and regulation of the qualities of production, prices, and personal consumption—sumptuary laws. These laws eventually died out, and only ghosts remained in memory and practice.

From the earliest colonial days down to the early nineteenth century, laws were passed attempting to restrict markets as to place, date, and time, enforced by local officials. It seems a very odd way to organize commercial activity to us, living in a society and at a time when shops are found in town and countryside alike, every day a market day, and some market days twenty-four hours long. These early practices seem oddly restrictive. For example, in Massachusetts in the 1630s and 1640s markets and fairs were established by law: "there shall henceforth be a market kept at Boston . . . upon the fifth day of the week from time to time, and at *Salem* . . . upon the fourth day . . . And at *Linn* upon the third day . . . And at *Charleston* . . . upon the sixth day. . . . It is also

Ordered and hereby Graunted to *Boston* aforesaid to have two Faires in a year, on the first third day of the third month, and on the first third day of the eighth month from year to year to continue for two or three days together." Similar fairs were set for Salem, Watertown, and Dorchester.[16] An annual fair was allowed in Brooklyn, New York, in 1675; a market house was established at the Battery in New York in 1676.[17] Philadelphia was allowed by its 1691 charter to hold two market days each week and three fairs a year.[18] New York City, with its staple right over all cargoes passing through the harbor, seems to have had a liberal practice of market days. In 1708 Annapolis was allowed to hold a market each week and a fair once a year. In 1745 Baltimore was given the privilege of holding two annual fairs, and Frederick-Town was allowed a market on Wednesdays and Saturdays.[19] The royal governor of South Carolina complained in 1724 that the assembly was usurping his prerogatives by establishing fairs and markets and appointing commissioners to preside over them.[20] Georgia in the mid-eighteenth century not only attempted to control commerce by the establishment of specific markets but even imposed the medieval injunctions against "forestalling, engrossing, and unjust exactions therein"—buying up goods before they reached the market or cornering the market.[21] As in English market towns, the place appointed for the market was soon the site of a piece of municipal architecture; the shape of the market house of Philadelphia was widely copied by interior cities in the early nineteenth century. The early nineteenth-century frontier towns, according to Richard Wade, "not only constructed market houses but also extended municipal regulation over a wide variety of trading activity. Ordinances protected the public against adulterated foods, false measurements, and rigged prices. Some municipalities went even farther and assumed responsibility for seeing that 'justice' is done between buyer and seller. In search of this objective officials fixed prices on some goods."[22]

---

[16]*Colonial Laws of Massachusetts*, p. 150.   [17]Brodhead, 1:289, 300.

[18]Allinson and Penrose, *Philadelphia*, p. li.   [19]Mereness, *Maryland*, pp. 414-19.

[20]W. Roy Smith, *South Carolina*, p. 85.   [21]Jones, *History of Georgia*, 1:479-85.

[22]Wade, "Urban Life in Western America," pp. 20-21; Bridenbaugh, p. 149.

This tradition is an outgrowth of the English law of the market overt and its practices, which originally included the self-regulation of merchants outside the proceedings of the royal courts, except on appeal, the laws of the merchants being applied in the courts of piepoudre, or piepowder (a medieval word for dusty foot, or itinerant traveler), where justice was dispensed on the very day the action arose. In fact piepoudre courts appeared in Maryland.[23] A law of Edward III in 1353 regarding these courts stated that the king's officers were not to interfere in the merchants' disputes, because "the merchants cannot often tarry in one place in hindrance of their business, we will and grant, that speedy right be to them done from day to day and from hour to hour."[24] Commerce in the early English law was considered an occasional thing; essentially an interruption of normal life, it was to be limited in its duration and restricted as to its influence. Such a conception developed from a medieval life primarily based upon agriculture, religious duties, and military service. As commerce grew, it was treated as an exception, first in borough life and then in the appointment of specific fairs and markets. Other commercial life was restricted mainly to such controlled enterprises as common houses and common callings, where what was sold, to whom, and at what prices was not left to the higgling of the market. Market prices were arrived at in markets only, duly appointed. A two-part problem was solved by this procedure: first, commercial interlopers were regulated, as were other business activities, and second, full title to goods passed when they changed hands. According to Blackstone the English solution to these problems came down from Saxon times. No title to goods valued above twenty pence could change hands among the Saxons without witnesses, just as were required for deeds or wills. The requirement of witnesses was assumed to be fulfilled if goods were sold in specified open markets, or markets overt. Commodities bought in open market had their titles protected; if money was paid and accepted "in earnest," the transaction could not be reversed. As long as the

---

[23]Blackstone, bk. 3, pp. 28-29; Mereness, pp. 420-21.

[24]Edward A. Adler, "Business Jurisprudence," *Harvard Law Review* 28 (1914-15): 139.

full price was eventually paid, legal title to the goods passed.[25]
This payment of earnest money was later set down in Charles II's
Statute of Frauds of 1677 (and continues to this day in our customs regarding purchase of real estate and consumers' durables).[26]
The authority to hold a market overt was vested in a person or a
town, and a clerk of the market (a subordinate, thought to have
been an ecclesiastical appointee originally) was the official who
regulated entry to the market, exacted the toll, and directed the
proceedings of the court of piepoudre in case of disputes.[27] Of the
court and its official, Blackstone said: "It is a court of record, incident to every fair and market; of which the steward of him, who
owns or has the toll of the market, is the judge. . . . The court hath
cognizance of all matters of contract that can possibly arise within
the precinct of that fair or market."[28] Because the sale of goods
took place within this jurisdiction and was to be a witnessed legal
transaction, it remained only to establish the places of the
markets. Blackstone explained the logic of the market system, although by his time, the mid-eighteenth century, these courts of
piepoudre were a thing of the past in England, where they had
once been the most commonly held of all courts.

But property may also in some cases be transferred by sale, though the
vendor *hath not* [property] *at all* in the goods; for it is expedient that the
buyer, by taking proper precautions, may at all events be secure in his purchase; otherwise all commerce between man and man must soon be at an end.
And therefore the general rule of law is, that all sales and contracts of any
thing vendible, in fairs or markets *overt* . . . shall not only be good between
the parties, but also binding on all those that have any right or property
therein. . . . for this purpose . . . were tolls established in markets, *viz.*, to
testify the makings of contracts; for every private contract was discounte-
nanced by law. . . . Market overt in the country is held only on special days,
provided for particular towns by charter or prescription; but in London every
days, except Sunday, is market day. The market place, or spot of ground set
apart by custom for the sale of particular goods, is also in the country the
only market overt, but in London every shop in which goods are exposed
publicly to sale, is market overt, for such things only as the owner professes
to trade in.[29]

[25]Bk. 2, pp. 362-63, 365. [26]29 Charles II, c. 3, art. 17. [27]Blackstone, bk. 2, p. 275.
[28]Bk. 3, pp. 28-29.   [29]Bk. 2, pp. 364-65.

It was for these reasons that the colonists originally established market towns, days, and fairs in their little settlements. In a predominantly agrarian society, where there were few facilities for storage and the sources of commodities were largely domestic and close at home, such a medieval conception of commerce as a necessary disturbance to be controlled within a larger social framework was sensible enough. But the colonial society soon became one of extensive settlement, with commodities shipped between colonies in bulk and overseas. Legality of transactions limited to local arrangements only made little sense. By the end of the seventeenth century in New England farms were allowed to sell directly to customers outside the market days and places, and by the early eighteenth century the colonists were objecting to limited market days. The people in New Hampshire "complained that so much produce coming in at one time would glut the market and place the sellers at the mercy of townspeople."[30] Farmers had to wander through a town to sell goods and might end up with losses because of the necessity to sell at the end of the day. A specialized merchant community developed, and more and more cities had to be reckoned as market towns and seaports, where customs were collected and goods warehoused.[31] The carefuly controlled English system of limited markets became obsolete.

Urban trade underwent the same transformation. At first, when most trade was either bespoke with individual craftsmen or at established markets, emerging retail trade was seen as a threat to established order, and it was outlawed in the 1660s in Connecticut and Virginia.[32] Moreover, a specialized merchant community in the towns had the precedent of London, and later other major

[30]Weeden, *Economic and Social History of New England,* 1:406, 2:524-26. Bridenbaugh cites evidence of opposition by country people to Boston's somewhat fitful efforts to maintain their market overt (pp. 194-95).

[31]On markets overt, fairs, and the steady emegence of a mercantile community outside the English system as it was first established in the colonies, see Bridenbaugh, pp. 27-29, 41-42, 180-81, 192-93, 334-36, 349-54, 355. Saposs cites efforts in Virginia in the 1660s to protect established markets by prohibiting retail trade (in Commons et al., *History of Labor,* p. 40). On ports and customs, see *Colonial Laws of Massachusetts,* pp. 158-60, 200; Weeden, 1:373; Brodhead, 1:318; Allinson and Penrose, pp. 25, 109; Mereness, pp. 91, 417-18; and Bridenbaugh, pp. 23-23, 171.

[32]Saposs, in Commons et al., *History of Labor,* p. 40.

English towns, where every shop was a market overt whose sales were legal, and every day, save Sunday, was a market day. Apart from restrictions on the legality of sales to Indians and a few relics of open markets in certain towns, with their officers, clerks, and wardens renting stalls to sellers for a fee, the system largely passed into history even before the end of the colonial era. One remnant showed up in the lengthy dispute between the Philadelphia journeyman cordwainers and their masters that was set off in 1789 when the masters' association ruled that no shoemaker who sold out of his shop "in the public market of this city" could be elected for membership.[33] The cordwainers by then had a retail and custom trade of their own, and so the competition of the established market was resisted. The journeymen formed their own association in 1794, and when they struck against their masters in 1805, the decline of the open market, the specialization of the master as a seller and manufacturer, and the place of the journeymen as employees came into focus.

By the late eighteenth century it had become accepted American legal doctrine that the English law of markets overt did not apply in this country.[34] The practices of medieval commerce died out under the more dynamic requirements of an utterly commercial society. The rule of *caveat emptor,* or buyer beware, also a part of the common law, generally proved a substitute for the market overt in America. *Caveat emptor* did not protect against all fraud, but it left the seller unencumbered regarding the buyer's gullibility if any defect in the commodity was open to observation, "where attention would have been sufficient to protect him from surprise or imposition."[35] There still existed a whole set of common-law conventions running from straight market sales through auctions to storage, delivery, hiring, and pawnbroking under the law of bailment covering the physical movement of things bought, rented, or stored, so that the colonist and frontiersman were not left without protection from the rapacity of merchants by the disappearance of the English constraints upon retailers.[36] But within the infinity of local zoning and licensing ordinances merchants were free, for the most part, to buy and sell without the whole apparatus of the witnessed transfer of title

[33]Commons et al., *Documentary History,* 3:128.   [34]Kent, 2:417-18.
[35]Ibid., pp. 654-705, esp. pp. 670-71.   [36]Ibid., pp. 317-78.

which characterized and was the purpose of the old open market. In some towns one still finds the colonial relic, the farmers' market day; and where passage of title is taxed, as in automobiles, the hand of the Middle Ages still lies upon the transaction and the clerk of the market takes his toll.

Even with the passing of retail sales as a strictly local phenomenon under firm scrutiny, the custom of municipal quality control continued for half a century in the older states like Pennsylvania and Massachusetts. Beginning with the Food and Drug Act of 1906 and the Federal Trade Commission in 1914, the federal government entered this area of nonmarket control. One cannot avoid being struck by the vigor with which our ancestors attempted to protect the citizen from the cupidity of sellers. It is clear that the forces of free-market competition played little role in early colonial thought. Again, acquaintance with a competitive market for goods, as in the market for labor, was probably too limited for such ideas to develop. Faith in the market economy to regulate itself by competition came only with experience and the ideology of classical economic theory, probably reaching its fullest development in the United States before the Civil War. This belief in the virtues of laissez faire was a mental exercise which came concurrently with a recognizable actuality. When the market worked, people believed; when it did not, faith began to wane. After the Civil War, when the free market seemed to develop defects, there followed demands for federal nonmarket social controls in agriculture, industry, banking, transport, and in modern times such controls threaten once again to become ubiquitous.

Because applying the free market to foreign competition never appealed to American manufacturers, in this area there was always explicit nonmarket control. After the comprehensive English controls under the Acts of Trade and Navigation were eliminated by the Revolution, the tariff was substituted. The early colonists, when they bought from the English or Europeans, could depend upon Old-World quality controls, either because such commodities were made under the ubiquitous European system of guilds or because there were official controls over trade from non-European sources, such as the government-sponsored trading monopolies in commerce with the tropics. There was as yet no industrial revolution in Europe to remove manufacturing from the person of the craftsman. In the early colonial days, when guilds had not yet been set up in America, quality control of domestic output was a natural demand. The colonial laws of Massachusetts are filled with such controls; leather, wood, fish, grain, and the processing, packing and shipping of them, were set under strict regulation. The controls were to be enforced by the constables, viewers, gaugers, wardens, reefs, and so forth, appointed to oversee the output of each commodity. To fix the more general public interest, rewards for confiscated goods, or splitting of fines, commonly included the informer in the distribution. These laws covered weights, measures, and workmanship.[37] A typical law of the mid-seventeenth century states:

And for the preventing deceit on any person in the packing of fish, beef, and porke to be put to sale . . . in every Town . . . the Gager or Packer of that Town, or of the Town wherein it is put to sale or shipped, shall see that it be well and orderly performed: that is to say: beef and porke, the whole halfe or quarter, & so proportionably that the best be not left out, and for fish, that they be packed all of one kind, and that all Casks so packed be full and sound and seasoned. . . . if such goods so packed shall be put to sale without the Gagers mark he shall forfeit the said goods, that puts them to sale, the one halfe to the Informer and the other halfe to the countrey."[38]

It would be difficult to conceive of a more effective procedure, or one more unpopular with producers. The public was rewarded for finding violations of the law. Such restrictions fell upon virtually all goods produced for sale. These laws commonly included controls of prices as well; in 1646 a fairly ingenious sliding-scale bread price system was enacted.[39] There never seems to have been any doubt of legal authority to enforce such laws in England or the colonies, and indeed the general powers are given in Magna Carta.[40] In context, controls of quality and prices were akin to local control over paupers, alms, charity, and orphans and were a

[37]*Colonial Laws of Massachusetts*, pp. 72, 124-25, 126, 129-30, 152, 157, 168-70, 175, 184, 191-92, 199, 200, 227-28, 243; Allinson and Penrose, pp. xlvi-li, 51, 131, 137; Brodhead, 2:71-75, 330; Jefferson, *Notes*, p. 223; Bruce, *Economic History*, 2:424-25; Mereness, pp. 109-117; Bridenbaugh, pp. 202, 356. For a discussion of the English origins of all these laws, see Powell, *Puritan Village*, ch. 3.

[38]*Colonial Laws of Massachusetts*, p. 130.   [39]Ibid., pp. 124-25.

[40]Magna Carta, art. 35, in Bagley and Rowley, p. 106.

settled part of the colonial scene. Hence Philadelphia's laws in the 1770s regulated the sizes of casks for meat-packing and prices "for the better settling of the markets" and required "the sellers of meat and grain under the court house to open the mouths of sacks . . . that the inhabitants may see what they buy.[41] Specific price control laws go back at least to 1349 in the reign of Edward III; colonial assemblies passed them; and during the American Revolution no less than eight of the thirteen states enacted comprehensive price control laws. Any American president or legislature that attempts to control prices has a long set of precedents to draw upon. As Oliver Wendell Holmes said in 1905, due process was not defined as laissez faire, and "the Fourteenth Amendment does not enact Mr. Herbert Spencer's Social Statics."[42] Modern advocates of consumer protection thus are also squarely in the American tradition. It might be added, as a cautionary note, that the Revolutionary price-control laws were disastrous failures. The colonial quality-control laws seem to have been stopgap measures taken before guilds, and then competition in selling goods, imposed discipline upon those who made them. The idea of rewarding informers who spy out defective merchandise, part of the colonial heritage, has not caught on again, although the government does reward income-tax informers.

How much of the colonial output was effectively regulated by such laws is unknown. It seems clear enough that the disappearance of the system of open markets must have made any effective general regulation more difficult. Although the tradition continued, if weakly, in the business history of Massachusetts and Pennsylvania in the federal era,[43] and purely civic controls were maintained in American towns by local ordinance, the disestablishment of New York's system by constitutional amendment in 1846 indicates that the first installment of American consumerism had become a dead issue in that state by then. The fading of detailed nonmarket control in Massachusetts by the mid-

[41]Allinson and Penrose, p. 51.

[42]"Notes," *Harvard Law Review* 33 (1919-20): 838-40. Bridenbaugh gives an extensive review of colonial price-control efforts (pp. 45, 49-52, 151, 197, 198, 202).

[43]Handlin and Handlin, *Commonwealth,* pp. 68-72, 93-94, 219, 220-21, 260-62; Hartz, *Economic Policy and Democratic Thought,* pp. 4, 204-7.

nineteenth century has been described by the Handlins: "It was as if, imperceptibly, all the familiar metes and bounds that marked off one man's estate from another vanished to leave a vast and open space. . . . Somewhere everyone knew, the state could act directly. . . . But where one field ended and another began, no one knew; the master map was not yet drawn."[44] Recently many master plans have been drawn, at all levels of government, and the metes and bounds are still hard to locate. The problems are generally the same as those of the colonial era, but they now are far more complex in detail.

Regulation of personal expenditures on clothing existed in New England alongside the quality controls over production in the seventeenth century, but they apparently died out by the eighteenth century. Laws governing expenditures on personal apparel, or sumptuary laws, go far back into English history. It is thought that they originally were meant to discourage the importation of luxuries and to protect personal estates from profligacy. Since they also typically regulated personal opulence on the basis of social rank, these laws seem also to have been intended to encourage social cohesion. In medieval towns dress was commonly a sign of rank; our modern academic paraphernalia are a survival of such practices. By the time of Henry VIII, English society was pulling away from such minute regulation of personal consumption. His laws repealed, then reimposed, then repealed the sumptuary restrictions. Mary reimposed part of the old law in prohibiting the use of silk by most persons, but this was probably a blow at France. All sumptuary laws appear to have been lifted in a law of the first year of the reign of James I,[45] but in 1651, when the Puritans and their ideas about abstinence were triumphant in England, the Puritans of Massachusetts imposed such a law.[46] This

---

[44]P. 260.

[45]1 Henry VIII, c. 14, was "A repeal of all former statutes against excess of apparel; and what kind of apparel men of all degrees and callings are allowed, and what prohibited to wear"; 6 Henry VIII, c. 13, reimposed the ancient laws. 7 Henry VIII, c. 6, repealed them again, as did 24 Henry VIII, c. 13. 1 and 2 Phillip and Mary, c. 2, prohibited wearing of silk except for mayors and aldermen. 1 James I, c. 25, repealed all sumptuary laws. For a general survey of English practices, see Frances Elizabeth Baldwin, *Sumptuary Legislation and Personal Regulation in England* (Baltimore, 1926).

[46]*Colonial Laws of Massachusetts*, p. 123. There had been an earlier sumptuary law in Virginia (Morgan, "The First American Boom," p. 179).

American act was strictly class legislation, as were the medieval sumptuary laws. The law was not to "extend to the restraint of any Magistrate, or publicke Officer, their wives and Children, who are left to their discretion in wearing of apparel, or any settled Military Officer or Souldier in the time of Military Service, or any other whose education and imployment have been above the ordinary degree, or whose estate have been considerable, though now decayed." The burden of the restriction was thus meant to fall upon the common citizen. The reasons given for the law were both moral and economic: "we cannot but to our grief, take notice, that intolerable excess & bravery hath crept in upon us, amongst people of mean condition, to the dishonour of God, the scandal of our profession, the consumption of estates, and altogether unsuitable to our poverty." Anyone whose estate was less than £200 was prohibited from wearing such items as gold or silver lace or buttons, expensive bone points, and silk hoods or scarfs. The law was to be enforced at the township level: "the Selectmen of every Town, or the major part of them, are hereby enabled and required from time to time, to have regard, and take notice of apparel of any of the Inhabitants . . . and whosoever they shall Judge to exceed their rankes & abilities in the costliness, or fashion of their apparel in any respect, especially in the wearing of Ribbons or great boots . . . lace, points . . . silk hoods or scarfes, the Selectmen aforesaid shall have power to assess such persons."

In 1662 the law was embellished with the comment that "the Rising Generation are in danger to be corrupted and Effeminated."[47] These laws were widely adopted in New England, especially in Connecticut, and efforts to enforce them extended at least into the 1670s.[48] Their eventual failure was no doubt due to the rising standard of life, the difficulties of enforcement, and the general waning of the Puritan faith as the rigors of the early days faded from memory. Apart from laws concerning sexual practices, these sumptuary laws were probably the limit of the colonial attempts to excercise social control over economic life through the regulation of personal behavior, unless one wants to argue that the

[47]Ibid., p. 220.

[48]Weeden, 1:286-89; Bridenbaugh, pp. 97, 412. Bridenbaugh cites a Massachusetts ordinance of 1712 which even attempted to limit expenditures on funerals.

laws against such things as drunkenness, "lewd dancing," and sing-
ing in taverns were of economic origin. I would forbear advancing
such an argument. Today the colonial sumptuary laws are little
more than historical curiosities. Most of our severely puritanical
religious movements (and even political movements) have utilized
sumptuary restrictions to enforce the faith,[49] as do Mennonites,
Hutterites, and the Catholic clergy even in the midst of modern
affluence. The spirit of the sumptuary laws seems to linger on in
the speeches of politicians about the consumption habits of "welfare chiselers."

Another area of traditional nonmarket social control was that
of common callings, or what we now consider public utilities,
regulated industries, and licensed enterprises. Here *caveat emptor*
has never prevailed, from colonial times to the present day. We
know this form of control best in industrial America because of
the controls over systems of transportation that became prominent in the late nineteenth century in the form of federal regulation of basic transport and communications systems under the
powers of the Federal Constitution's commerce clause. It is important to emphasize that however shaky the Sherman Antitrust Act
of 1890 prohibiting restraint of trade might have been in the
common-law framework, the Interstate Commerce Act of 1887,
which put the railroad system under federal regulation, had an
ancient lineage, in the colonies and in England before that.

In 1630 a franchise was given for a ferry between Charlestown
and Boston.[50] The rates and services were set by the government.
By that time public regulation of common callings was already
three-and-a-half centuries old in English law. The first statute
appears to have been one of Edward I in the year 1285 under
which suits were allowed against persons in public businesses who
failed to serve properly.[51] It is thought that such obligations originally applied to all persons who engaged openly in business to

---

[49]Examples are the austerity of early-day Brownshirts in Germany and Blackshirts in
Italy, the bogus peasant blouses and uniforms without insignia of Stalinist Russia (before
Stalingrad), the homogeneous blue boiler suits of Communist China, the mock worker
get-ups of the middle-class American New Left enthusiasts of the late 1960s and early
1970s.

[50]Weeden, 1:110.

[51]Burdick, "Origin of Peculiar Duties of Public Service Companies," esp. p. 515.

serve the public.[52] This theory would tally with the fact that there
was extensive control of prices in the old system of restricted
markets. Certain trades connected with long-distance trading,
including those of innkeepers, public "victuallers," porters, draymen, ferrymen, coachmen, boatmen, brewers, and "sellers of
strong waters," attracted to themselves the idea of a public obligation to serve all who applied, in a workmanlike manner, and at
reasonable or even fixed rates. In cases where a public monopoly
or franchise was given, the power to regulate was not questioned,[53] but recognition of the obligations of the common carrier
appeared even before franchises were extensively granted. In cases
falling under the common law of bailment, which included public
obligations of pawnbrokers, innkeepers, wharfingers, and common
carriers, the public's control was established very early in English
legal history.[54] Cases are known in the fourteenth century in
which common carriers are regulated. The records of the York-
shire town of Beverley contain extensive documentation on this.
For example: "Also it is ordered by the keepers of the town of
Beverley in the Gild Hall of Beverley, at an assembly of the whole
community, S. Wilfrid's day A.D. 1367, and to this all the porters
and creel men of Beverley who then commonly exercised that
right in Beverley consented, that each of them should take for the
load or baggage of one horse from Beck to the Minster and East-
gate 1/2 d; from the Beck to Cross Bridge 3/4 d." In the same year
the control of beer prices was reenforced by an order that "if any
one offer 1½ d for a gallon of beer anywhere in Beverley and the
ale wife will not take it, . . . the purchaser comes to the Gild Hall
and complain of the brewster, and a remedy shall be found." Controls in Beverley in the fifteenth century included even the
sequence in which common carriers were to accept business if
several persons applied simultaneously.[55] It is possible that these
sorts of businesses associated with long-distance trade were subject
to controls over common callings because their business lay
between those local jurisdictions, where business control was

[52]Adler, pp. 140-42.   [53]Burdick, pp. 518-23.

[54]Blackstone, bk. 2, pp. 367-70. On American adaptation of English law in this
regard, see Kent, vol. 2, all of Lecture XL.

[55]Burdick, pp. 527, 528, 531 n.83.

easier and limited to certain places and days. The same logic would apply to innkeepers, who served a traveling public, and indeed in colonial Massachusetts travelers themselves were largely exempt from a town's full control if they were at inns.[56] Little business was exempt from nonmarket control in England before the sixteenth century, and the special obligations adhering to common callings may have stuck to those engaged in or on the borders of long-distance trade simply because no easier method of control was possible: they were operating between, not within, the local jurisdictions. It is clear that the idea of natural monopoly did not have to apply for such control to exist. Out of this control arose the peculiar obligations of persons in common callings and the origins of our public regulations of utilities, railroads, airlines, and taxis.[57]

The impact of this background is apparent in colonial law and practice. In Massachusetts not only was the innkeeper's business regulated but the innkeeper himself also came under critical scrutiny. In 1641 the records show that William Davis "was denied libertie to sell drinke, or ale, or to keepe a cookes shopp, because there are others sufficient in the towne of Boston, and his carriage hath been formerly offensive." Not only was beer-making restricted to those properly trained in the "art or mystery of brewing," but anyone who bought beer found to be "unwholesome or useless" got his money back. In 1647 innkeepers and others selling drink were ordered to "hasten . . . to their several imployments and places of abode" young people, "whether servants, Apprentices, Schollers belonging to the Colledge [Harvard] or any Latine schools," found idling in such places. To keep innkeepers from giving credit to sailors, it was ruled that such debts could not be recovered in courts. The colony had a comprehensive set of laws regarding innkeepers and public houses that included controls of quality, prices, and maximum consumption per customer. A supply of "strong wholesome beer" had to be on hand at not more than twopence a quart. Taverns within a mile of meetinghouses had to be cleared during meeting times, except for "strangers."

---

[56]*Colonial Laws of Massachusetts*, p. 166 n.12.

[57]See the Handlins, pp. 103-20, 222, 255-56, on continuance of such controls in Massachusetts in the federal period; for Pennsylvania, see Hartz, pp. 259-60.

Innkeepers were even required to provide for horses.[58] Inns set up throughout New England were under similar controls. The constables were from "time to time" to "duly make search" to enforce the laws. Licenses were renewed only from year to year. In New York similar regulations existed for inns. In Virginia the courts licensed taverns and also fixed their charges. The same was true in Maryland.[59]

Common carriers were considered to be public utilities from the beginnings of the colonial experience. Ferries, established before bridges, were controlled regarding fees and service. In Massachusetts, the sequence of services rendered, as in fourteenth-century Beverley, was specified. The right to refuse service was granted if the ferryman or "the most of the passengers first entered" were so inclined. Medical persons "called to women's labours" got first place on Massachusetts ferries, and traveling magistrates paid no fares[60]—a portent, perhaps, of free passes for politicians on railroads in a later era. As in fourteenth-century Beverley, the Massachusetts elders imposed restraints upon other common carriers too: "There being a very great abuse in the Townes of Boston and Charlestown, by Porters, who many times do require and exact more than is just and righteous . . . It is ordered . . . the Select men of said Townes . . . shall have power to regulate." Colonial Philadelphia had similar regulations of "carters, draymen & porters," as did New York. In Virginia, according to Jefferson, "ferries are admitted only at such places as are appointed by law, and the rates of farriage are fixed."[61] These sorts of controls of common carriers, the product of common law and English statute law, became a part of the tradition of colonial, and then American, social control. The same was true of franchises. Monopolies were granted, under strict control, to operate toll bridges in certain

[58]*Colonial Laws of Massachusetts,* pp. xiii, 126, 137, 190-91, 165.

[59]Weeden, 1:112-13, 207, 313; *Colonial Laws of Massachusetts,* p. 166; Brodhead, 2:71-75; Jefferson, p. 253; Mereness, p. 353. See also Bridenbaugh, pp. 44, 113-15, 156, 197, 198, 268-74, 354-55, 426-35.

[60]*Colonial Laws of Massachusetts,* pp. 150-51. For establishment of ferries and control of rates in New England, see Weeden, 1:110-11, 114, 205-6, 211, 311, 2:511, 879.

[61]*Colonial Laws of Massachusetts,* p. 185; Allinson and Penrose, p. 51; Kent, 2:802-30; Jefferson, p. 253.

places.[62] It is significant that two of the momentous cases in the history of American constitutional law grew out of these practices. New York's grant of a franchise to Robert Fulton to monopolize steam navigation on the Hudson River resulted, ultimately, in *Gibbons* v. *Ogden* in 1824, the definitive Supreme Court test of the commerce clause.[63] The *Charles River Bridge* case in 1837, when it was decided that Massachusetts could grant a corporate charter to a toll bridge in competition with an earlier and similar grant,[64] was instrumental in paving the way toward general grants of incorporation in the American states, and away from the English tradition of corporate powers implying monopoly privileges as well as the obligations of franchise.

The points of contact with the external world, the seaports of colonial America, were also points of taxation not only for the colonies but for the crown as well, and their regulation was from the beginning a settled matter. The entire apparatus of English law regarding the ports came over with the colonists, remained throughout the colonial period, and was adopted by the American states and then by the federal government in its courts of admiralty jurisdiction. James Kent noted that the maritime laws passed by Congress in 1792 and 1793 controlling foreign trade, coasting trade, and fisheries were little more than copies of English law as it existed during the reign of George III.[65] Our rules governing ports and shipping articles (contracts of seamen)[66] and our

[62]Weeden notes a toll bridge established at New Milford, Conn., in 1756. The first New England bridge he finds in 1633, paid for by Boston and Roxbury. It is not certain which of the earlier New England bridges were free and which toll. Some were built by township labor and taxation (1: 207-13).

[63]9 Wheaton 1 (1824). The long-run significance of Marshall's decision is discussed in Robert L. Stern, "The Commerce Clause and the National Economy, 1933-1946," *Harvard Law Review* 59 (1946): 674-78.

[64]James Willard Hurst, *The Legitimacy of the Business Corporation* (Charlottesville, Va., 1970), pp. 38-39; Kent, 3:614 n.(a).

[65]Kent, 3:Lecture XLII on maritime law: first American admiralty laws, pp. 198-99.

[66]Ibid., Lecture LXII; for congressional laws governing shipping articles see esp. pp. 244-45. Before the Revolution the laws of the colonies were those of England; the admiralty courts tried cases of both colonials and Englishmen without any signs of discrimination, at least in the printed record (see Reginald G. Marsden, ed., *Reports of Cases Determined by the High Court of Admiralty and Appeal Therefrom . . ., 1758-1774* [London, 1855], pp. 20-23).

customs regarding charter parties (rental of ship space) were all inherited from the English. One interesting difference involves ownership. English shipowners were joint tenants with a fairly restricted property right. Americans took over the more liberal idea of the sleeping partner (a limited partner with no vote) from Louisiana, and it was quickly adopted throughout the United States.[67]

Thus we find in connection with general laws of contract, markets, and control of common callings that colonial America was anything but a hotbed of laissez faire philosophy. Colonial America was in fact the child of English mercantilism. It was only in 1776, as the American colonies were finally revolting against (among other things) the strictures of Britain's international mercantilism, that Adam Smith, in *The Wealth of Nations,* launched a broad theoretical attack against the whole idea of ubiquitous nonmarket social control of economic enterprise. So it is not surprising to find such controls of business as thickly "on the ground" of colonial America, just as were the conditions of labor.

While the colonial economy's expansion both geographically and in volume rendered much of the early system obsolete, a great deal of it remained, and some of it was destined to return. For example, the legal position of organized labor embodied in the idea of craft or guild, the exclusive right to practice a "mystery" in a given place, came back again in the form of legally established labor unions in the 1930s. Outside of the prison system, unfree labor disappeared, one hopes, forever. The public control of markets, which included pervasive quality controls of manufacturing and processing in colonial times, appeared at the federal level early in the twentieth century, expanded slowly but steadily, has become widespread again in our own time, and reformers want more of it. Social control of common callings never disappeared; inns, canals, wharfs, and public houses were always controlled where settled communal life came into existence. But in modern times, beginning with railroads and the enormous proliferation of the communications network, the powers of public control, under the infinitely spreading umbrella of the commerce clause,

[67]Kent, 3:34, 42-43.

developed an unprecedented impact. *Gibbons* v. *Ogden* was the beginning of a trend which has already had nearly revolutionary consequences for American capitalism. Even the colonial ideas of controlling prices of farm commodities and production returned with a vengeance in the twentieth century, when the social system finally attempted through the federal government to solve the problems of American agriculture. The conditions of the frontier led some of the English institutions of control, products of a relatively static society, to fade or change. Others, such as licensing and other municipal controls, remained in existence. But in the twentieth century, with the frontier long gone and America attempting in its own right to become a more ordered society, our present-day efforts to find solutions to economic, and therefore social, problems are creating nonmarket controls that bear a strong family resemblance to the colonial past.

In those areas where central government and domestic economic life were always closely conjoined—money, taxation, and foreign trade—the economic break with the past was more apparent than real when the new republic took power. Names of things changed more than did the things themselves.

10

Prometheus Partly Bound:
The Colonial Money Genius

Thus far we have concentrated our attention upon the forces of nonmarket social control at the lowest levels of communal economic life. No doubt colonists felt the pressure of communal constraint upon their lives most constantly at that level, within the broad domestic network of laws and customs. The government of crown and Parliament may have seemed far away, remote. But running through the whole texture of colonial economic life were the needs of government. Local government was supplied with resources from domestic taxation. This taxation could be as primitive as the corvée, the conscription of labor, animals, and materials to work on roads, bridges, and other public works, or it could raise the funds to pay and equip military and constabulary forces.[1] Colonial governments also laid duties on imports to provide for government needs which were not covered by local taxation or votes of moneys by the colonial assemblies. Crown and proprietary officials tried to collect quitrents where they were due, claimed a share of prizes and wrecks where appropriate, and collected general customs where possible.

All these efforts combined to constrain and channel colonial economic activity in directions in which more than the direct private interests of the colonial economy were served. The colonists were subjects of kings and queens whose officials directed the affairs of a sprawling and growing empire. The various governments in London groped with their problems, and the colonists had to live with the consequences or try to evade them. Even in modern times, with modern communications and knowledge, such an endeavor would be (and has been) loaded with crippling complexities. In colonial times it is really inconceivable that a mutually satisfactory system could have been found between the

---

[1]*Colonial Laws of Massachusetts*, pp. 134-35; Mereness, *Maryland*, p. 353; W. Roy Smith, *South Carolina*, pp. 283-84.

objects of imperial policy and the desires of the colonists. In fact, it is astonishing that the colonies acquiesced in crown policies as much and as long as they did. Inertia and fear of the Indians, the French, and the Spanish must have played as large a role as tradition says they did. It is clear that even at the start of the hostilities in the 1770s complete independence was not a universally accepted objective. It is not so much that colonial status was a direct economic burden to the colonies; it probably was not. But so many options were effectively closed to the colonists, which they fervently wanted open. They wanted freer access to land, to foreign markets, to local fiscal control. If they were well off in the empire, they might be better off under different circumstances, or so many came to believe. In many ways the most pointed indicator of these conflicts of interest and policy arose in the narrow sphere of currency, and the meaning of the phrase *the shortage of money.*

It is useful here to be a historian as well as an economist, to consider the facts in literary evidence as well as the theoretical justification of such an idea. Economists have spilled an ocean of ink over this issue. The initial problem lay in the clouded definition of *money.* If that meant a ready supply of English coin circulating in the colonies hand-to-hand, the colonists complained that they did not have enough of it.[2] Exportation of English coin was illegal,[3] and when it was melted into bullion and shipped out,

[2]Some colonies had more English coin than did others, depending upon the direction and net balance of their trade. Massachusetts, by the late seventeenth century, New York, and Pennsylvania seem to have been better supplied with coin than others, especially exclusively agricultural colonies like Virginia. Will and estate inventories showed little coin among assets in Virginia during most of the seventeenth century, and in Virginia tobacco was accepted in payment of quitrents as early as 1645. In an effort to reduce claims on uncultivated land in 1682 the Virginia governor ordered quitrents on holdings over 1,000 acres to be paid in coin, a clear indication that it most likely could not be done by any but the most wealthy. The Virginia records are filled with testimonials regarding the "money shortage" (Bruce, *Economic History*, 2:507, 543, 560-61, 499-501). In Massachusetts wampum was declared to be tender for private debts up to 40 shillings in 1643 (*Colonial Laws of Massachusetts*, p. 198), and by 1654, as we noted above, rules were defined for payments of contracts in kind. The problem of English coins and colonial needs is discussed in Curtis P. Nettels, *The Money Supply of the American Colonies before 1720* (Madison, Wis., 1934), pp. 162-78; Roger W. Weiss, "The Colonial Monetary Standards of Massachusetts," *Economic History Review* 27 (1974): 577-92.

[3]Nettels, p. 162.

it was more likely to go to Europe or Asia than to America. The colonial economy was not a significant producer of the metals used to make coins. So colonial coinage was a limited and irregular affair.[4] Paper money was created, backed by colonial government IOU's, mortgages, or even faith alone. Paper issues were resisted by conservative colonial interests as well as by the crown. The price of money, the legal rate of interest, was set by usury laws,[5] and so there was no question of speculative shipments of coins to the colonies to take advantage of interest differentials, even if such a venture could be considered a serious proposition with the primitive communications of the time. Since the colonies had no real banks or other financial institutions, it is in any case not certain who might have offered the necessary interest premiums, were they possible within the limits set by usury laws.

What was left then as a source of money, considered only as coin, was the net gain in trade between the colonies and Europe or Spanish and Portugese America. The evidence of widespread use of Spanish and Portugese coins indicates some success in the latter area, but the per capita supply of coins must have been very low in the early colonies. The majority of new immigrants, indentured servants or slaves, can have brought little coin with them, and the colonists' complaints throughout most of the colonial period referred to the shortage of coins; moreover, since coins bore premiums in trade, they were no doubt hoarded as well. What the colonists used as media of exchange in lieu of coins was wampum, grain, skins, tobacco,[6] or just book credits defined in such terms or warehouse receipts exchanged for commodities stored, negotiable paper, IOU's, the irregular emissions of debt instruments of

[4]Massachusetts established a short-lived mint in 1652 (*Colonial Laws of Massachusetts*, pp. 181-82; Nettels, pp. 171-75). Copper coins were apparently minted in Connecticut in the early eighteenth century (Nettels, p. 175). See also Channing, *History of U.S.*, 2:496-500.

[5]The maximum legal interest rates were no doubt governed by the English maximum rates, which drifted downward throughout most of the colonial period. The maximum rate allowed in Massachusetts was 8 percent (*Colonial Laws of Massachusetts*, p. 39). In Virginia by the early 1780s the rate had fallen to 5 percent (Jefferson, *Notes*, p. 223). Such laws could be circumvented, of course, by paying premium prices in local produce for coins, and this was in fact the universal practice and was a primary reason for the devalued colonial pound against the English pound.

[6]Nettels, pp. 202-28.

colonial governments, and any other substitutes that came to hand. It was not a case where shortage of money meant that transactions could not take place, but rather that transactions were complicated by the inappropriateness and inconvenience of the multitude of "moneys" used. In fact, considering the small number of people involved, the history of money in colonial America is a tribute to the ingenuity of the human animal; it is complicated beyond all reason.

The idea of a money shortage being just lack of coins was complicated by another problem. Conflated with the lack of coin was the feeling of producers in an economy devoted largely to primary production that adverse terms of trade (low prices of domestic goods relative to prices of imports) resulted somehow from the debtor position of an economy growing rapidly enough to require more imports, decade after decade, than its exports could easily pay for. Such beliefs appeared early in colonial history. But they were not, after all, peculiar to the colonial era. The cry for cheap money as a solution to low prices and incomes in the primary sectors of the economy was heard through the antebellum period, the greenback era, the Populist and free silver movements, the New Deal to yesterday's newspaper. The debtor almost always wants more money cheaper than the creditor is willing to supply. That is one reason why the rate of interest is always a positive number. Hence it is no paradox that the colonial farmer, like his Populist descendant, could be both a hard money and a cheap money enthusiast. It is also not surprising that the colonial debtors resented efforts to interfere with their cheap money schemes, just as their descendants would object to similar efforts by the First and Second Banks of the United States, the National Banking System, and the Federal Reserve System—efforts to impose some limit on the supply of money less than the needs of commerce or what have you demanded. The control of money exercised by the crown in colonial times was both a governmental constraint upon economic activity and the beginning of a long and complex history of currency and banking controversies which continue to the present day. Through the Revolution, the Confederacy, and the federal era flowed the incessant desire of America's frontier settlers to get credit cheaply in an easily negotiable form which they called money; coins were most desirable, and paper money was the most possible. In one form or another colonies succeeded in issuing paper money. This legacy, despite the paper money disasters of the Revolutionary era, lived on.

If money is considered to be a commodity, and its creation a production process, then all aspects of its market were subjected to continued attempts to impose government regulation—nonmarket control—throughout the colonial period. The number of issuers (producers) was severely restricted; entry was made difficult or impossible (the Massachusetts land bank, the death penalty in Pennsylvania for counterfeiting); the maximum price was fixed by usury laws; and many complex efforts were made to control the quality of the money produced.

At first, when trade was local, the money used could be of local circulation only. When trade was with wampum-using Indians or persons who in turn traded with such Indians, wampum (beads made of clam shells) was money. There was no lack of sophistication about that money. It was first introduced from New Amsterdam by de Rassiéres into Massachusetts in 1623, and the whites soon understood, by trying to make wampum themselves, a fundamental law of economic life, comparative advantage. They could acquire wampum more cheaply by expending their labor on acquiring food and goods to trade for it than by cutting and polishing clam shells themselves.[7] The whites got wampum cheaper applying their own technology than by adopting that of the Indian, and the Indians in turn got goods cheaper by making wampum and trading skins for it than they could by adopting the technology of the whites. Here the money supply was determined by trade and productivity, and the element of collective social control was at its minimum. Wampum also provides an early colonial example of Gresham's law at work and of one of the first monetary reforms in American history. In New Amsterdam in 1641 unstrung wampum beads had driven the superior version, strung wampum beads, from circulation. The Dutch governor, Wilhelm Kieft, ordered a 50 percent appreciation of the Dutch money against unstrung wampum. This effectively devalued the Indian currency which had been debased (unstrung beads) in trade with the Dutch. The strung wampum, being no longer under-

[7] Goodwin, *Pilgrim Republic,* pp. 305-6.

valued, returned to circulation.[8] One presumes that Kieft was a clever man, that the price elasticity of demand for Dutch goods was less than one, and that as a result the Dutch realized a considerable gain in the returns from trade with the Indians, until the unstrung wampum disappeared.

The colonists could attract foreign coin if their trade goods were desired by foreigners, and more so, if they offered competitive premiums for coins in sterling values. This was tried, and the same foreign coins thus brought different sterling prices in different colonies.[9] Since no English coins were offered in exchange, the effectiveness of these competitive devaluations depended upon demand for the products of the colonies in question, and hence they could not solve the problem of coin shortages in all colonies. Coins were minted in Massachusetts and Connecticut and were purposely made light in metal relative to their nominal values in order to keep them from being exported. In addition, Massachusetts provided penalties for exporting coins and searchers to watch for coin smugglers and rewards for informers. In 1704 a standard set of exchange rates between colonial sterling and foreign coins was laid down by a proclamation of Queen Anne.[10] This set of exchange rates, called proclamation money, merely added to the complexity, since the colonies continued with their own foreign coin prices. In nominal units these practices meant that the colonial pound was devalued against the English pound; the amount of devaluation depended upon trade and coin prices between each colony and the outside world and varied from time to time. In the end the Spannish milled dollar of 1728 became the most popular coin in circulation; it was adopted by Congress in 1786 as the standard for American money.[11]

The devaluation of the colonial pound against sterling was also a product of colonial issues of official debt instruments which were used as money internally. Adam Smith and David Ricardo both considered the inflations that accompanied these debt issues to be evidence of their unsoundness, Smith because they were usually not redeemable at face value on demand, and Ricardo

---

[8]Brodhead, *History of State of New York,* 1:314.

[9]Nettels, pp. 229-42.   [10]Ibid., pp. 242-49.   [11]Channing, 2:498.

because too much was issued.[12] It was Benjamin Franklin, though, in his pamphlet *A Modest Inquiry into the Nature and Necessity of a Paper Currency*, who made the eternally usable statement about the supply of money with beautiful ambiguity: "There is a certain proportionate quantity of money requisite to carry on the trade of a country freely and currently; more than which would be of no advantage in trade, and less, if much less, exceedingly detrimental to it."[13]

In their issues of debt instruments the American colonists were real pioneers. Nothing quite like it was previously known among European peoples. The colonial governments needed to make payments in anticipation of tax receipts and in lieu of them. The desire of debtors for cheap money and the needs of colonial governments to spend in excess of their current receipts coalesced to produce our first uses of government debt as money: a discovery of unimaginable potential, leading straight to the present monetary uses of the federal government's debts and the great inflation of 1971-75.

Massachusetts led the way in 1690. At least as early as 1676 Massachusetts had borrowed from individual merchants, giving certificates of indebtedness of the colony's treasury which could be passed hand to hand like bills of exchange among the merchants.[14] As we have already seen, their laws enhanced and protected the contractual rights involved. Other colonies had also borrowed from private persons in a similar manner. In 1690 soldiers returning from the unsuccessful· expedition against Quebec could not be paid in coin. Massachusetts simply issued general promises of the government to pay, and the soldiers accepted them. When the government began accepting the notes back at face value plus 5 percent, they passed current as money.[15] Other colonies followed this practice: South Carolina in 1703, Connecticut, New York, New Hampshire, and New Jersey in 1709, Rhode Island in 1710, North Carolina in 1712.[16] In colony after colony

---

[12]Smith, *Wealth of Nations*, p. 310; Ricardo, *The Principles of Political Economy and Taxation* (London, 1908), p. 344.

[13]Quoted in Channing, 2:530.   [14]Nettels, p. 251.   [15]Channing, 2:500.

[16]Ibid., pp. 500-507; see also Nettels, ch. 10, on the early paper money issues, and Weiss on elements of stability in the system in Massachusetts.

the innovation was seized upon. Pennsylvania joined in 1723, conservatively, but by 1767 the gentle Quakers had legislated the death penalty for counterfeiting.[17]

The arguments justifying paper money were based on more than just government convenience. It was found that issues of money made trade more animated, and profitable, since prices tended to rise. It was also discovered that fixed obligations tended to be easier to pay in these circumstances. Colonial governments found that the money was made more acceptable if sinking funds were set up for ultimate redemption or backing was specified in unsold public lands and if bills carried an interest premium. If the colony declared that such notes were acceptable in payment of taxes, or were legal tender, the notes circulated even more readily. It was also found that if the supply of this money was reduced, the opposite chain of events tended to follow. So there was not only enthusiasm for new issues and agitation for their continuation but demands for more from those who stood to gain. Since the latter included the colonial governments, opposition from sound money interests and the crown was fitful and inconclusive.[18] These paper money issues continued up to the Revolution, when they were joined by a national paper currency and one of history's rarer events, a hyperinflation. The colonists had stumbled upon a philosopher's stone, the technique whereby all modern governments are able to make their current expenditures exceed their incomes and gently tax the public for the difference. With its paper money, colonial America was one of the prodigies of history.

No doubt the best-known effort to create paper money in the colonies was the Massachusetts land bank scheme of 1740.[19] Mortgages were accepted as assets of the bank in exchange for its

[17]Channing, 2:514 n.3. The death penalty for counterfeiting had already been applied in Philadelphia in 1720 (Bridenbaugh, *Cities in the Wilderness*, p. 222).

[18]Richard A. Lester, "Currency Issues to Overcome Depressions in Pennsylvania, 1723 and 1729," reprinted in *New Views on American Economic Development*, ed. Ralph Andreano (Cambridge, Mass., 1965). A summary of colonial paper money issues is given in *Historical Statistics of U.S.*, tables Z-359-70.

[19]Channing, 2:505.

own liabilities, notes, to be redeemed in twenty years in commodities. Those who exchanged their mortgages for the notes agreed to accept the notes for debts due. So although not declared to be legal tender, the notes enjoyed a wide circulation. This ill-starred enterprise was another breakthrough into modern financial practice, except that there was no reserve currency to be held as backing for the notes. Since many of the colonial paper money issues had declined sharply in exchange with coins and were associated with domestic price increases, the sound money interests were against the bank, and in 1741 they successfully induced Parliament to declare that the Bubble Act of 1720 (a law prohibiting private joint-stock companies) applied to the colonies. The 1741 law, "An Act for Restraining and Preventing Several Unwarrantable Schemes and Undertakings in His Majesty's Colonies and Plantations in America," effectively destroyed the Massachusetts bank.[20] With its treble damages, fines for violators, and compulsory sterling convertibility with interest and damages, the act made the land bank notes prohibitively expensive to issue.

The crown had also attempted to limit or constrain other colonial issues, without great success, and the record shows that despite all efforts to curb the creation of a domestic paper currency before the Revolution, the colonies in fact continued their circulation. The crown's contribution to this developing tradition was probably limited to the idea that paper money issues should somehow be restrained. That much came naturally enough to the colonial creditor interest, in any case. Gouverneur Morris of Pennsylvania stated conservative fears in the Constitutional Convention of 1787 in his discussion advocating imposition of executive review over the laws of state legislatures: "Emissions of paper money, largesses to the people—a remission of debts and similar measures, will at some time be popular and will be pushed." But in the discussion concerning prohibition of paper money, reality entered the debates. George Mason of Virginia argued for the colonial and Revolutionary experiences. He "had doubts on the subject. Congress he thought would not have power unless it were expressed. Though he had a mortal hatred to paper money, yet as

[20]14 George II, c. 37.

he could not foresee all emergences, he was unwilling to tie the hands of the legislature. He observed that the late war could not have been carried on, had such a prohibition existed."[21]

In the event, the Constitution forbade the states from issuing paper money themselves but did not prohibit issues from other sources, and they became the stock-in-trade of private banks in the federal period. The federal government was given the general power to borrow money and to coin it and regulate its value. Also, the new government took over the debts of the Confederacy.[22] These were sufficient powers to carry a long future. Madison, in *The Federalist Papers,* thought that the prohibition against the states' issuing paper money "must give pleasure to every citizen, in proportion to his love of justice and his knowledge of the true springs of prosperity."[23] One wonders how he would view the Federal Reserve note of our own era?

Hence the fruits of the colonial experience with money, both the knowledge of the benefits of paper money to governments and debtors as well as the resistance to it from those who controlled loanable funds in the private sector, passed into the mainstream of American experience. The monetary history of the United States may be seen as variations upon the theme established in colonial times. Governments, including the crown, both opposed and favored money creation, depending upon the circumstances, and to the present day this ambivalence has made a virtue of necessity. We have policies of monetary ease and restraint depending upon which interests gain the upper hand at a given moment, and such was true in the colonial era. The colonists opened a Pandora's box with the question, How much should the supply of money be?

[21]*Documents Illustrative of the Formation of the Union,* pp. 425-556.

[22]U.S. Constitution, art. 1, sec. 8, and art. 6.

[23]No. 44 of *The Federalist Papers* (New York, 1961), p. 281.

11

Trade and Navigation:
The Old System Sticks

IT IS commonly written that among the causes of the American Revolution were the intolerable burdens of the British laws governing colonial trade and navigation. The precise amount of the burden is a much-disputed subject. A legitimate separation of these laws can and should be made for our purposes. First there were certain basic laws and practices dating from early colonial times which seem to have been congenial enough to all parties. We will treat these shortly. Second was the series of acts of Parliament, beginning with the Molasses Act of 1733 and including a long list of laws to which the colonists objected vehemently: the Sugar Act and the Currency Act (prohibiting colonial paper money from being declared legal tender) of 1764, the Stamp Act of 1765, the Declaratory Act of 1766 (declaring parliamentary power to legislate for the colonies), the Townshend Acts of 1767, the Revenue Act of 1770, the Tea Act of 1773, and the Boston Port Act, the Administration of Justice Act, the Massachusetts Government Act, and the Quebec Act of 1774. All these and more make a list familiar to the student of American history. They gave rise to colonial resistance and revolution, and left little behind as a permanent legacy. Many of these acts were cited chapter and verse in the Declaration and Resolves of the First Continental Congress in 1774 and the Declaration of the Causes and Necessity of Taking Up Arms in 1775, and the contents were generally covered again in the Declaration of Independence. There can be little doubt how the Congress and the people felt about these laws.

But it should be recalled that apart from the Molasses Act of 1733,[1] which was largely evaded, this second group of laws was the product of Parliament in the final decade before the Revolution. For nearly a century and a half before that the colonies had

[1] A. M. Schlesinger, *The Colonial Merchants and the American Revolution* (New York, 1918), pp. 42-43.

been ruled by another set of laws which had controlled their external affairs and had not provoked armed resistance. These laws were the acts of Trade and Navigation of 1660 and 1663, the establishment in 1696 of the Board of Trade, and the extension in the same year of the powers of the High Court of Admiralty to American waters.[2] These acts, and even the ill-fated effort of James II in 1686 to create the Dominion of New England under Edmund Andros, defined the empire as more than a number of disconnected overseas settlements,[3] and they did leave a permanent residue in American history. It is often argued that these laws gave rise to little protest because they were only irregularly enforced. But since they also protected American merchants as well as English merchants from foreign interlopers, and from pirates as well, it is also probable that their success was in part due to their being mutually agreeable.

The act of 1660 was largely a reenactment of an act of 1651 passed when Cromwell was building an empire overseas. It stated that no commodities could be shipped into or out of the colonies except in English (which always included colonial) ships whose crews were at least three-quarters English and whose masters were subjects of the crown. English and colonial ships might trade with foreign countries and colonies provided they did not land any of a long list of enumerated colonial commodities, including tobacco, sugar, cotton, indigo, and ginger. These were reserved for the English market. In 1662 it was enacted that apart from prizes of war, only English-built (again including colonial) ships could ply the empire trade (although exceptions were made by naturalizing foreign-built ships). An act of 1663 made it illegal to trade European goods directly to the colonies without first landing them in England and paying duties (to be refunded if the goods were reexported). England itself thus assumed the sort of staple right over colonial trade that the Dutch West India Company had given New Amsterdam over cargoes passing its harbor. It was a curiosity in English law. An act of 1673 forced ships to pay a plantation tax

[2]George Louis Beer, *The Old Colonial System, 1660-1774* (New York, 1912), vol. 1, chs. 2-3; Andrews, vol. 4, chs. 3-4.

[3]Beer, 2:325.

on enumerated commodities loaded in the colonies and to post a bond against unloading these outside the colonies and England.[4]

Adherence to these acts and evasions of them alike set up the basic external growth pattern of the colonies, and the internal reactions to these stimuli shaped domestic economic growth. Adherence determined the extent to which colonial development was complementary to British development; evasion, the extent to which alien strains entered the pattern of growth. Apart from encouraging a spirit of independence among some colonial merchants (men like John Hancock, bold smugglers), neither the effects nor the amount of that evasion can be accurately measured. Even before the 1760s it is supposed to have been extensive. The admiralty courts certainly assumed by the 1760s that evasion was common, and the evidence of their proceedings seems to indicate that, as one judge put it in 1767, by smuggling the Americans were in fact attempting to "rid themselves of the Navigation Act."[5]

Both American merchants and crown officials understood that smuggling was the automatic reaction to excessive duties on goods imported into the colonies. A. M. Schlesinger, Sr., argued that the strength of the smuggling tradition was such as to build into the colonial system a long-term element which would have been hostile to the navigation acts even had the magnification of control in the 1760s and 1770s never occurred.[6] Both the controls of the navigation laws and the smugglers' reactive preference for a free market molded the developing pattern of external trade. This became clear after independence: Britain continued to be the major American trading partner when this trade represented free choice rather than empire solidarity, and nothing is better evidence of the system's long-term effectiveness. The old bond was not broken by the Revolution. In the first confrontation between the king and the victorious rebels, George III told John Adams, the newly appointed American ambassador, that if the United

[4]Andrews, *Colonial Period*, 4:61-63, 85-117, 77-82, 108-15, 119-22.

[5]Marsden, *Reports of . . . High Court of Admiralty*, p. 41. In this volume two cases, *Brown* v. *Kenyon* and *Freemason*, provide good insights into the techniques used by American ship captains to "run" cargoes without paying duties and carrying contraband. Both cases were heard in 1767.

[6]Pp. 59-60.

States was willing to give Britain "the preference," he was willing to pick up the pieces and try to build a new relationship.[7]

Control of colonial affairs by the Board of Trade after 1696 seems to have contributed at least four elements to the American tradition: (1) the idea of judicial review, (2) strong admiralty courts, (3) effective customs controls, and (4) central government control of overseas trade and commerce between the states. We have mentioned the element of judicial review before. It was an outcome of the indirect way in which the government in London ruled the colonies for so long.

The colonial assemblies acted under the injunction that the laws not be repugnant to the laws of England; so it was necessary that the colonial statutes be examined by experts in England and either approved or disallowed. The Board of Trade (and its prececessors), as an appendage of the Privy Council, undertook this examination, passing its recommendations on to the king in council. Of those statutes disallowed, over four hundred from 1696 to the Revolution, the most numerous were those that concerned credit, money schemes, stop laws, and bankruptcy laws.[8] Hence, Gouverneur Morris's advocacy at the Constitutional Convention of executive review of such state laws was based on a long experience. The board's review of colonial laws was entirely professional,[9] and its usefulness made a profound impression on the colonists even though by the eighteenth century such a procedure was foreign to the English constitution. That constitution was made by Parliament; the colonial constitution was held together and made uniform with it by the Board of Trade's review of colonial laws.[10] In the debates at the Constitutional Convention in 1787 the explicit idea of higher review, and even federal judicial review of state laws, was prominent, and its colonial origins were well understood.[11] It was left to the Supreme Court, in *Marbury* v. *Madison,*

[7]John Adams, *Works,* ed. Charles Francis Adams (Boston, 1853), 8:255-59.

[8]Dickerson, *American Colonial Government,* pp. 227, 252-53, and ch. 5 generally.

[9]Ibid., p. 234.

[10]The Beards concluded generally that the U.S. Constitution was in fact a reestablishment of the colonial constitution on a new federal basis (*Rise of American Civilization,* 1:202-3, 328, 340), a view which has not won universal acclaim over the years.

[11]*Documents Illustrative of the Formulation of the Union,* pp. 174-75, 178, 225, 242, 390-91, 423-33, 438-39.

to include the laws of Congress itself under the review of the courts.

An understanding of the usefulness of strong admiralty power was apparent in the new admiralty courts set up by the states after independence and then in the admiralty jurisdiction given to the federal courts in connection with the commerce clause of the Federal Constitution. The English admiralty courts had colonial jurisdiction from 1696 onwards, and became notorious in the 1770s for their intrusion into internal colonial affairs.[12] But before then, in the scattered colonial settlements along the Atlantic seacoast, these courts played a vital role in adjudicating disputes of all sorts arising out of the shipping trade and problems of wages and insurance.

A new Board of Customs Commissioners was introduced in 1767, along with the other acts designed to increase the crown's revenues. These laws must be counted successful as tax measures, and the board was one of those later imperial innovations whose impact remained. Before 1767 Americal colonial customs were said to have yielded less than £2,000 a year at a collection cost of nearly £9,000, certainly an unimpressive record. The Townshend Act raised and expanded import duties and set up the Board of Customs Commissioners, to be resident in the colonies, at first in Boston. From 1768 to 1774 the new duties raised perhaps £30,000 a year at a cost of £13,000. There was also a sixfold increase in the value of seizures of smuggled goods and ships.[13] The new customs service was enormously unpopular in the colonies and has always been counted among the causes of the American Revolution. Yet the colonies immediately imposed customs of their own after independence, the power was provided in the Federal Constitution, and the revenues were of fundamental importance in financing the federal government in its early years. The colonies had learned a valuable lesson from the detested Townshend reforms.

[12]Andrews, 4:222-33.

[13]Ibid., pp. 217-21; Channing, *History of U.S.*, 3:85-91; Dora Mae Clark, "The American Board of Customs, 1767-1783," *American Historical Review* 45 (1940): 772.

The power to collect customs was related to that of controlling commerce. No sooner were they able, after the Revolution, than the states imposed tariffs and taxes upon each other's goods and trade. Nothing short of civil war could have been more disrupting to the union of the new nation. There was much discussion and critical comment about this development at the Constitutional Convention; the commerce clause was the result.[14] In the colonial period the Board of Trade had regulated such matters, and it provided a clear precedent to remedy the chaos of the Confederacy.

As early as 1725 it became practice at the board to recommend disallowance of colonial laws that imposed discriminatory duties or regulations between the colonies.[15] The power to regulate commerce granted to the federal government by the Constitution has become, in the fullness of time, perhaps the single most powerful instrument of economic control in the United States. It has molded our history powerfully. Its modest colonial beginning is worth noting.

Since it was believed that the navigation acts had successfully stimulated the growth of the British merchant marine, it was not unnatural that American statesmen, successors to the British crown, would reenact the relevant legislation. In the first American navigation acts of 1792 and 1793, all ships deemed American had to be registered in American ports, as was the case of English ships in English ports before the Revolution. Kent said of these laws, "The object of the registry acts is to encourage our own trade, navigation, and ship-building, by granting peculiar or exclusive privileges of trade to the flag of the United States, and by prohibiting the communication of those immunities to the shipping and mariners of other countries."[16] No ship could be registered as an American vessel unless it was owned wholly or in part by an American citizen and sailed under an American master. The rules were the same for vessels licensed only for coastal waters and

[14]Nos. 42, 45, *Federalist Papers*, pp. 267-69, 292.

[15]Dickerson, p. 249. Evidence of such practice, adverse to intraempire trade, was the tariff of 10 percent imposed by New York in 1684 upon goods imported from other colonies (Brodhead, *History of State of New York*, p. 408).

[16]*Commentaries*, 3:197.

fishing. Such ships could not go to sea without acquiring a registration, as was also the case in English law before the Revolution. Penalties for violation were heavy. In 1813 Congress even prohibited, at least in law, employment of foreign seamen on American ships. Foreign ships could enter American ports from foreign ports upon payment of alien duties.[17] Coastal and inland shipping was reserved to American ships.

Although not so severe as the English laws in some respects (we did not demand that American ships be American-built or prizes of war), the inspiration of the British navigation laws was direct. As Kent blandly put it in his own evaluation of these laws in 1826, "The Acts of Congress of 31st December, 1792 and 18th February, 1793, constitute the basis of the regulations in this country for the foreign and coasting trade, and for the fisheries of the United States; and they correspond very closely with the provisions of the British statutes in the reign of George III." Kent was also amused to see the alacrity with which the laws and rules of English admiralty courts had been adopted by U.S. courts in 1801-15, demonstrated in Cranch's *Reports* of cases brought before the U.S. Supreme Court: "It is curious to observe in these reports the rapid cultivation and complete adoption of the law and learning of the English admiralty and prize courts, not withstanding these courts had been the constant theme of complaints and obloquy in our political discussions for the fifteen years preceding the war."[18]

As for the foreign trade itself, the new nation followed closely in the mercantilism of its parent. Although the first tariff act, of July 4, 1789, was partly aimed at revenue, its long list of protected goods testifies to the American manufacturer's appreciation of this income-diverting technique. The act begins piously enough: "Whereas it is necessary for the support of the government, for the discharge of the debts of the United States, and the encouragement and protection of manufactures, that duties be laid on goods, wares and merchandise imported. . . ."[19] There was no question of free trade or free-market allocation of resources.[20]

[17] Ibid., 3:197, 199-203, 249-50.

[18] 3:198-99, 1:503.

[19] *United States Customs Laws, 1789-1895* (Washington, D.C., 1896), p. 9.

[20] Nor was there undiluted enthusiasm for trade without protection of all sorts at the meetings of the first Congress under the Federal Constitution. Protectionist senti-

Foreign trade was an instrument of the state from the beginning. Massachusetts had once passed laws providing for free trade, in 1645. The law was unusual at the time, and was certainly repugnant to the laws of England: "all ships which come for Trading onely, from other parts, shall have free access to our Harbours, and quiet Riding there, and free Liberty to depart without any Molestation by us." But the colony's immediate problem was to generate external trade during the period of the Protectorate. Once the Acts of Trade and Navigation took over, the problem was to limit foreign trade according to the interests of overall imperial policy. Accordingly, in 1661, after the Restoration, Massachusetts laws were changed to enable enforcement of the navigation laws.[21] The realization of free trade as a national policy was limited mainly to nineteenth-century England, and was never part of American colonial life, apart from early Massachusetts and certain promises of trade freedoms in early charters. Trade was controlled until 1776 in the interests of empire, and from the beginning of the federal period the overall policies of the national government, aided and abetted by vested interests, determined this country's commercial policies.

Hence in shipping and in commercial policy the colonial experience produced a continuing tradition. Considering the "bad press" the British navigation laws have always had in American history books, these facts are both amusing and enlightening, for we see the comparative success of the infant American government in its external commercial efforts as the product of practical experience, and not successful innovation.

Americans saw their own empire just as the British had seen theirs. The difference was one of perspective. The American empire was primarily a concentrated landmass with coastal and inland waterways from which foreigners could be easily excluded. The old British empire had been a worldwide assortment of commercial nodal points held together by seaways common to the ships of all nations. To enforce solidarity, the British developed

---

ment was strong at the beginning of the federal period; see E. A. J. Johnson, *The Foundations of American Economic Freedom* (Minneapolis, 1973).

[21]*Colonial Laws of Massachusetts,* pp. 192-220.

the old colonial system based upon the laws of trade and navigation. The Americans, well aware of the system's success, adopted
parts of it for themselves when their time came. Number, entry,
prices, and quality were all controlled in the new republic's
interests. Here, as in so many other areas, what seemed characteristically American in the new republic was in fact the colonial
experience conscripted from the pre-Revolutionary past to serve
again. In both eras the object of nonmarket social control of external economic relations was to divert the flow of economic
resources from those which might have prevailed in free-market
conditions to those channels which served apparent political and
politico-economic realities. This use of central government for
social control objectives was a time-tested system by the end of
the eighteenth century. Hence it was not the use of government
power vis-à-vis the external world that was novel in the new republic. The apparatus, laws, and personnel of early American ports,
customs, docks, wharfs, lighthouses, and shipping registries were
all in accord with British and European practice and law. Where
the new republic developed a surprising novelty was its use of
government for social control objectives in its internal economic
development.[22] But that came in new circumstances, when the
continent's interior was American, and not British, Spanish,
French, or Indian.

---

[22]See Carter Goodrich, *Government Promotion of American Canals and Railroads*
(New York, 1960); Handlin and Handlin, *Commonwealth*; Hartz, *Economic Policy and
Democratic Thought*; Milton S. Heath, *Constructive Liberalism: The Role of the State in
Economic Development in Georgia to 1860* (Cambridge, Mass., 1954); and Hurst,
Legitimacy of Business Corporation.

Part IV

Live Hand of the Past

12

Nonmarket Control, an American Tradition

> When the people of the United Colonies separated from Great Britain, they changed the form, but not the substance, of their government.
>
> Chief Justice Morrison Waite, 1877

Chief Justice Waite has been considered by some legal scholars to have been excessively idiosyncratic in his opinion in *Munn* v. *Illinois*.[1] In that decision Waite ruled that the state of Illinois had the power to regulate warehouse charges by virtue of an essay, *De Portibus Maris*, written by the seventeenth-century common-law jurist Sir Matthew Hale. The decision in *Munn* was the major decision in the Granger cases, all handed down in 1877, which validated, among other things, state laws regulating railroads.[2] These were fateful decisions, as the railroads fought against the new doctrine, and its overthrow in their favor in the *Wabash* case[3] a decade later gave us the Interstate Commerce Commission. In *Wabash* the Court held that railroads were interstate commerce, and under the Federal Constitution, only Congress could regulate interstate commerce. It did so a year later by passing the Act to Regulate Commerce, which established the ICC. With that law American history began to come full circle, the new commissioners playing the federal version of New England's regulating selectmen. Our mass of regulatory agencies is the direct institutional exfoliation of the ICC. We did not have major federal

---

[1] 94 U.S. 113 (1877). See Adler, "Business Jurisprudence;" Breck P. McAllister, "Lord Hale and Business Affected with a Public Interest," *Harvard Law Review* 43 (1930): 759; Maurice Finkelstein, "From Munn v. Illinois to Tyson v. Banton, a Study in the Judicial Process," *Columbia Law Review* 27 (1927): 769; Gustavus H. Robinson, "The Public Utility Concept in American Law," *Harvard Law Review*, 41 (1928): 277.

[2] *Munn* v. *Illinois; Chicago, Burlington and Quincy Railroad* v. *Iowa; Peik* v. *Chicago and Northwestern Railroad; Chicago, Milwaukee and St. Paul Railroad* v. *Ackley; Winona and St. Peter Railroad* v. *Blake.*

[3] *Wabash, St. Louis and Pacific Railway Co.* v. *Illinois*, 118 US. 557 (1886).

regulatory agencies before the ICC, and we have not been without them since. With the appearance of the ICC, the federal government began to exercise those kinds of direct regulatory powers enjoyed by colonial governments a century earlier.[4]

As a matter of fact, Waite was not being so idiosyncratic, as Professor Harry Scheiber has recently shown.[5] Hale's doctrine that private property "affected with a public interest" was, in common law, subject to public control had been widely cited in state courts before *Munn.* The tradition of nonmarket control at the state level had remained unbroken, and it was a living tradition to which Waite applied for dialectical ammunition. As Waite argued in *Munn,* such powers had been used "in England from time immemorial, and in this country from its colonization to regulate ferries, common carriers, hackmen, bakers, millers, wharfingers, innkeepers . . . and in so doing to fix a maximum charge to be made for services rendered, accommodations furnished, and articles to be sold. To this day, statutes are to be found in many of the States upon some or all of these subjects; and we think it had never yet been successfully contended that such legislation came within the constitutional prohibitions against interference with private property."[6] A century of independence, Waite argued, had not changed these basic powers. The substance of American government in these matters was the prerogative to regulate private business. Events since 1877 have not proved Waite wrong, except that he was too conservative. Oliver Wendell Holmes argued later in a minority opinion,[7] and in the *Nebbia* case in 1934 the Supreme Court agreed with him, that government has the power to regulate any business it wants to, affected with a public interest or not.[8]

---

[4]Massachusetts had pioneered the development of permanent public service commissions at the state level early in the federal period (Handlin and Handlin, *Commonwealth,* pp. 255-57).

[5]"The Road to Munn: Eminent Domain and the Concept of Public Purpose in the State Courts," *Perspectives in American History* 5(1971): 329.

[6]95 U.S. 113 (1877).

[7]*Tyson* v. *Banton,* 273 U.S. 438 (1926): "The truth seems to me to be that, subject to compensation when compensation is due the legislature may forbid or restrict any business when it has sufficient force of public opinion behind it."

[8]291 U.S. 502(1934): "It is clear that there is no closed class or category of businesses affected with a public interest."

Some areas of economic life had never been free of federal controls, foreign trade and land policy, for example. One form of business, at least, had been broken by the federal military power, Negro slavery. During the Civil War banking began to come under the federal power with the National Bank Act of 1863. Other federal influences were felt in railroad construction and financial control in the Thurmond Act of 1878. Conservation efforts came within the Timber Culture Act of 1873 and the Desert Land Act of 1877. Yellowstone Park, established in 1872, was the first of a whole system of parks, forest, and preserves set aside from commercial exploitation by the market mechanism. In 1890 business organization itself was added to the federal domain with the Sherman Act, again, it was always said, following the logic of the common law of England (interpretation of that act has certainly made a mighty contribution to judge-made law). A decade later the Gold Standard Act reestablished federal power in an area of economic life which had been partly freed of it by the monetary consequences of the Civil War. Previously the Sherman Silver Purchase Act of 1878 and the Bland-Allison Act of 1890 had placed a government subsidy under silver production. These acts were precursors of a time when subsidized production would effectively numb the market mechanism in fundamental parts of the economy. Yet the crown had also encouraged precious metal discoveries. It was not a new idea.

Bit by bit the structure of federal nonmarket control was pieced together. The Pure Food Act came in 1906, after the scandals of the food industry were exposed by Upton Sinclair and the muckrakers. Following the Panic of 1907 and the resulting National Monetary Commission, the Aldrich-Vreeland bill of 1911 gave private banks federal warrant to issue fiduciary money in times of emergency. Then, with the Democratic victory of 1912 the Progressives accelerated federal nonmarket power under the banner of reform, and in 1914 came the Clayton Antitrust Act, the Federal Trade Commission Act, and the Federal Reserve Act. In 1916 the federal farm loan banks were established. In 1876, the year before *Munn*, there was very little federal regulatory power. By 1914 the federal government's three divisions were flanked by major and permanent nonmarket control bureaucracies, all of them motivated and assisted by Congress, the courts, and the presidency.

With the First World War the continuous crises of twentieth-century life commenced. World War I, the stock market crash in 1929 and depression of the 1930s, the New Deal with its numberless nodes of federal economic power, World War II, the Fair Deal, the Korean War, the Cold War, the Vietnam War, the Nixonian phases, and the energy crisis and stagflation of 1973-75—all these crises were met by further constructions of the bureaucratic apparatus of nonmarket controls, the Securities and Exchange Commission, the National Labor Relations Board, the Civil Aeronautics Board, the Federal Power Commission, and many, many more. Each period contributed something permanent, so that the American economy became encrusted with living pieces of its history in the shape of long-lived regulatory agencies. In every area of economic life accretions of federal power existed: foreign trade and international monetary relations, food production, education, control of the labor contract, the banking system and the capital markets, communications from surface mail to orbiting satellites, land, sea, and air transportation, the environment, the supply of energy, social security, medical care. From the production of butter to the production of steel, laws and control agencies governing the number of economic agents, participation in economic activity, prices of output, and the nature of products and services vended edged ever nearer to total coverage.

The fiscal revolution encouraged this kind of nonmarket control. The federal government establishment and its constantly expanding revenue needs were fed by payroll tax deduction, an automatic "check off" from the national income; so planning and spending agencies arose designed to produce spending policies that would generate the levels of income needed to support federal budgets. Economists were stationed in the White House itself after the Employment Act of 1946. This massive structure of nonmarket control over economic life became the official institutional framework of the American economy. The scope of the price mechanism as a social control system was reduced in many areas to mere arbitrage functions, marginal adjustments, within the levels of aggregate economic activity determined by the federal apparatus. Agriculture since the 1938 AAA has been the best-known example of this, but in 1973-74 Americans learned to their dismay about the Webb-Pomerene Act of 1918, the Connally Hot

Oil Act of 1935, the Bureau of Mines, the Texas Railroad Commission, and the presidential powers under the Defense Production Act of 1950, all of which determined the supply of oil in this country, not the market. By 1964, with the Administrative Conference Act, and then, beginning in 1968, the Administrative Conference of the United States under that act, this country had a protogovernment of government control agencies, an American *conseil d'état.*

Obviously all these developments are consistent with our whole tradition. Obviously there is no turning back. Politicians speak of the free enterprise system, mainly in election years, and economics professors lovingly sketch its theoretical dimensions on their blackboards. But it is freedom to engage in uncontrolled enterprise in the interstices, along the borderlines, in the cracks, beyond the pale. The main parts of economic life have their dimensions set by government agencies. This is called by some a mixed enterprise system; by others, neomercantilism. How one views it is largely a matter of value judgment. How much government does one prefer to have in his life? One thing is clear—the General Services Administration's annual tableau of independent and quasi-independent regulatory and control offices, commissions, councils, boards, institutions, authorities, services, and government corporations is not a blueprint of free enterprise capitalism—the private ownership and control of productive resources. Since the federal control structure was put together piece by piece over a century of history as responses to specific problems (some of which vanished so long ago that only historians remember them), our bureaucracy is not a planning system either. It is not socialism, as its enemies charge; it is just officeholding. It is a mammoth version of the British government in colonial times.

That government too had been the consequences of practical experience and institutional response to concrete changes. Sometimes, as in the disappearance of markets overt, in antebellum America, and in the 1920s briefly, the areas affected by the government controls shrank. But mainly, for most of the decades of our history, the tradition of nonmarket control has been in vigorous and growing evidence, for a century now at the federal level. It is a matter of proportions. One great value of our colonial economic history is its illustration that the vast dimensions of our modern nonmarket control system are no greater, relative to the sum of current economic activity, than were the control devices of the little colonial economy. John Maynard Keynes might be alarmed and appalled by the scope of our present system, but Benjamin Franklin probably would not be. Certainly the men who passed the colonial laws of Massachusetts three and a half centuries ago would find us surprisingly lax and permissive. By their lights our economy still has far to go to reach that "meet order" desired of their gaolkeepers.

Finally, to display the colonial precedents of our modern nonmarket system of control is not to defend them or their descendants, either morally or in terms of their triumphs or failings in economic efficiency. Such issues are far beyond the scope of this little book. Its purpose has been more modest, but perhaps this study explains why the stream of economic ideology is turbid in our time. It was muddy at its source.

Index

Index